# AWAKEN YOUR INTUITION

## Empowering Women
for
Success In Life & Business

New Orleans Psychic Medium
# CARI ROY

# Table of Contents

# PREFACE

How it all started for me…

On one long and hot summer evening in the sixties, at the tender age of eight, I stumbled upon an adventure so peculiar yet amusing that it marked my entry into the realm of psychic abilities and intuition. This is not just the tale of how I discovered my gift, but a story rich with the support and encouragement from my family—especially my mother, a talented psychic medium, and my grandfather, a master astrologer and numerologist.

It all began out in our garden. My curiosity piqued by a glistening butterfly, I reached out, only to be greeted by a sudden, clear vision—a big storm was on its way, ready to quench the earth's thirst and cause a little of an uproar. Confused yet intrigued, I shared this premonition with my mother, who was nearby, reading her tarot cards on an old tree stump.

Rather than dismissing my experience as mere child's fancy, she looked at me with eyes in earnest, "The world communicates with us in myriad ways, and you, little girl, are beginning to listen." Her words, warm and full of encouragement, nudged me gently towards embracing a gift I was only beginning to recognize.

As night fell and our family gathered for dinner, the sky, true to my vision, burst open and a tropical storm whipped up blowing down a tree and part of the fence. This was way before weather alerts and cell phones and there had been no indication our sunny weather would change. My grandfather, listening attentively at this time, glanced at me over his glasses, his face alight with pride. "It appears you've inherited the gift from us.," he said with a chuckle, "The cosmos is vast and full of mysteries, and it seems you're ready to tune in to its secrets."

In the years that followed, my mother and grandfather became my guides on this newfound path. They introduced me to the practice of meditation and journaling, the vibrant energy of crystals, and the cosmic ballet of the planets and stars, tarot, palm lines, mediumship, reincarnation and more. Our lessons were always infused with laughter—like when I attempted to meditate and ended up snoring, or the time I confused Mars for Mercury, much to my grandfather's feigned dismay as they are very different from each other.

My mother would share tales of her own early brushes with her abilities, like confusing a spirit's message with the grocery list, leading to a comically mistaken purchase. My grandfather recounted his own astrological blunders, like the time he inadvertently forecasted a baby boy instead of a girl which caused a bunch of redecorations by the parents although the date and time were correct. Even the very best of us can err sometimes and they helped me understand that. They taught me that a 75 to 80% accuracy rate is as high as can be expected and that that is pretty darned amazing. If you encounter someone who says they are 100% perfect, not only do they lack in humility, it just isn't possible.

But amid the laughter and light-hearted moments of my lessons, I learned something invaluable—the essence of trust. Trust in my own abilities, in the unseen energies of the universe, and in the loving guidance of my family. I came to understand that intuition was not merely about predicting the future or conversing with the unseen; it was about forming a deep connection with the world both around and within us.

This story, woven with humor and warmth, serves as a beacon of hope, reminding us all of the intuitive spark within us. Like me, with the right encouragement and practice, anyone can cultivate this gift, delving into the magical and mysterious embrace of the universe. And maybe, on this journey, we'll all discover moments of laughter, love, and profound connections, finding the ultimate treasure—learning the language of our souls.

# INTRODUCTION

Welcome, dear fellow seeker, to the start of a life-changing adventure—a divine invitation to discover the most sacred gift hidden deep inside you. My name is Cari Roy, and I am deeply honored to be your guide and friend on this exciting journey into the heart of your intuition. As a psychic medium and astrologer with roots in the magical city of New Orleans, I have dedicated my life to guiding others on their spiritual paths. This book, "Awaken Your Intuition: Empowering Women for Success in Life & Business," is a result of my life's work, aimed at unlocking the incredible power of intuition that lives inside each of us.

My own path was lit by the stars and the advice of my elders. My mother, a gifted psychic medium, and my grandfather, a master astrologer and numerologist, were my first teachers in the world of spiritual wisdom. They showed me how to listen to the universe's quiet messages, to understand the stories told by the stars, to trust the insights found in the numbers that surround us and listen to messages from spirit. Their guidance helped me to grow my own gifts, a family legacy of intuitive knowledge passed down through generations and it is my joy, now, to share it with you.

In the mid 1980s, I took a significant step in my career and began working at The Bottom of the Cup Tearoom in the historic and vibrant French Quarter of New Orleans. In this place, rich with history and culture, I began my work as a psychic medium and astrologer, helping people find direction and clarity. Those early years were crucial in sharpening my skills and deepening my understanding of the spiritual connections we all share. I came up with some of the very best readers in the city and am always indebted to them too in helping me cultivate my gifts. Driven by a desire to help even more people, I trusted my own intuition and went out on my own in 2000 and started my own business, reaching tens of thousands of lives at this point.

This book is a special invitation to you, especially to women who feel an inner call—a hint of untapped potential, a spark of power waiting to shine. Intuition is your natural right, a divine connection to the universe's wisdom. It is a gift that my family has cherished for generations, and I have spent my life perfecting, sharing, and now, teaching it.

You might ask, "Why focus on women?" Through my years of experience, I have seen how intuition uniquely lives in the feminine spirit. It is a key part of who we are, connecting us to the wisdom passed down by women throughout history. However, in our busy lives, this deep connection can fade. My goal is to help you find this inner voice again, to make it stronger so it can light your way in life and business.

Together, we will explore how to awaken and grow your intuitive powers, sharing stories of change, practical activities, and advice on making intuition your most trusted ally for success. This book is about more than discovering your potential; it is about taking back your power, realizing your value, and recognizing the incredible abilities you have.

As we step into the world of your inner strength, remember, this journey is as much about rediscovering as it is about awakening. Your intuition has always been there to guide you, sometimes quietly, sometimes loudly. Now is the time to listen, to nurture, and to let this deep wisdom guide you to a life of achievement, empowerment, and true happiness.

Let us start this amazing journey together, with open hearts and minds, ready to awaken the intuition that has always been inside you, waiting to be revealed. Welcome to "Awaken Your Intuition: Empowering Women for Success in Life & Business."

Big hugs and much love,

Cari Roy

# INTUITION BASELINE QUIZ

**H**ere is a fun and insightful quiz designed to help you uncover the strength of your intuitive abilities before we start! Remember, intuition is a natural part of being human, and everyone has intuitive potential. This quiz is crafted to ensure you feel encouraged about your innate intuitive talents. Let us find out just how in tune you are with your inner guidance!

1. When you meet someone for the first time, how quickly do you get a "feel" for their personality?

A. Almost immediately—I tend to trust my first impressions.

B. After a short conversation, I usually pick up on their vibes.

C. It takes me a while; I prefer to see how they act in different situations.

2. How often do you experience "gut feelings" about a situation or decision?

A. Very often; my gut is my personal advisor.

B. Occasionally, in moments of uncertainty.

C. Rarely, I rely more on facts and logic.

3. Have you ever thought of someone right before they called or messaged you?

A. Yes, it happens quite often.

B. A few times, and it always surprises me.

C. Once or twice; it seemed like a coincidence.

4. Do you tend to notice subtle changes in your environment or in people's moods?

A. Yes, I am extremely sensitive to the energy around me.

B. Sometimes, especially if I am paying close attention.

C. Not really, I might not notice subtle cues.

5. How do you make important decisions?

A. I listen to my intuition, even if I cannot fully explain my reasoning.

B. I consider my gut feeling, but I also look at the facts.

C. I rely mostly on analyzing the information and possible outcomes.

6. Do you often have dreams that seem to carry messages or insights?

A. Yes, my dreams are often vivid and insightful.

B. Occasionally, I will have a dream that feels significant.

C. Rarely, my dreams do not usually seem meaningful.

7. When learning something new, do you prefer to follow your instincts or a structured approach?

A. I go with my instincts and explore freely.

B. A bit of both; I like having some guidance but also trust my instincts.

C. I prefer structured, step-by-step instructions.

## Scoring:

Tally your answers and see how intuitive you are—but remember, in this quiz, everyone is a winner when it comes to intuition!

Mostly A's: Intuition Expert!

Your intuition is a powerful guide in your life. You are deeply in tune with your inner wisdom and often rely on it to navigate both personal and professional situations. Trusting your gut comes naturally to you, making you an intuition expert!

Mostly B's: Intuitive Explorer!

You have a good balance between intuition and rationality. You are open to exploring your intuitive feelings, especially when making decisions or reading situations. Your intuition is a tool you are learning to use more consciously, and you are on a great path of intuitive exploration!

Mostly C's: Intuition Novice!

You might rely more on logic and reason, but your intuitive potential is waiting to be unlocked! You are at the beginning of your intuitive journey, with so much exciting potential to explore. Remember, intuition can be developed with practice, so you are on your way to discovering a whole new side of yourself.

## Conclusion

No matter your score, remember that intuition is a skill that can be nurtured and developed over time. This quiz is just a fun way to celebrate your intuitive potential and get a base level understanding of how in touch with it you are from the start. Make a mental note as we are about to amp it up. Keep listening to that inner voice—it is one of the most valuable resources you have and we are going to develop it so you have it at your command at will!

*Chapter 1*

# UNDERSTANDING INTUITION

### *The Power of Intuition*

Let us jump straight into the mystical world where intuition is the ruling force, that incredible inner guide that belongs to each of us. It is more than just random gut feelings or quick guesses; indeed, intuition is the secret language of the soul, a vast reservoir of insight that guides us toward our true direction in both personal and professional lives. As we delve into "Awaken Your Intuition: Empowering Women for Success in Life and Business," we are set to discover the magical influence of intuition and its role as a guiding light for women on their journey to personal growth and career achievement.

For us women, intuition is a sacred gift, a flicker ready to be ignited and grown into a bright flame. This natural instinct is our beacon through the intricate journey of life and business, providing clarity and assurance when the external world seems to favor objective, analytical reasoning. Welcoming our intuition unlocks a wealth of inner knowledge, empowering us to make decisions that align with our true selves and deepest desires.

In this subchapter, we will explore how intuition can be a powerful ally, showing up in our feelings, physical sensations, and the quiet messages in our dreams. We will discuss how to cultivate a strong, trusting bond with our intuition, learning to listen to its guidance with steadfast belief.

Particularly for the entrepreneurs and career-focused women navigating the rapid streams of the business realm, intuition is your ace in the hole. Amid the dynamic exchange of ideas and opportunities, while logic holds its ground, intuition is that flash of brilliance that lights up new pathways, informing strategic moves and unraveling complex issues with its nuanced signals.

We are going to introduce sacred techniques and rituals to awaken and strengthen your intuitive senses, including meditation journeys, writing down the conversations of your soul, paying attention to the intelligence of your body, and interpreting your dream signals. By integrating intuition into all aspects of our lives and careers, we open up a universe of limitless possibilities, paving the way for achievements and satisfaction that exceed our greatest imaginings.

So, whether you are a spiritual seeker, a business innovator craving intuitive breakthroughs, or a pioneer in your field, this subchapter invites you to tap into the transformative power of intuition. Let us trust our inner voices, follow our passions, and unlock our intuitive capabilities for a life filled with purpose, happiness, and unmatched success.

## *Clearing the Air on Intuition Myths*

For starters, let us clear the air and illuminate the truths about intuition, shall we? In the magical domain of intuition, numerous myths and tall tales obscure our view, preventing us from recognizing the true essence of this divine navigator. As women, whether we are making waves in the corporate world, filling our homes with love, or embarking on spiritual journeys or epic adventures, it is crucial that we separate fact from fiction when it comes to our intuitive abilities. This subchapter serves as our beacon in the shadows, cutting through the fog surrounding intuition, and enabling us to fully acknowledge its grandeur in every aspect of our lives and careers.

First off, the notion that intuition is a rarefied gift for only a select few could not be further from the truth! Each of us, whether in the office or at home, possesses the spark of intuition. This inherent talent is simply waiting for our recognition and nurturing, ready to flourish without bounds.

Secondly, intuition is not merely a fanciful "gut feeling." It is a rich orchestra of our deepest insights, emotions, and the quiet murmurs of the world around us. This deep-seated consciousness goes beyond simple logic, linking us to a reservoir of subconscious understanding.

Third, we must debunk the idea that intuition is a whimsical, unreliable guide. On the contrary! Intuition moves beyond the strict confines of logic, offering us wisdom and foresight that might elude our rational minds. By blending intuition with our intellect, we forge paths toward decisions that are both smart and aligned with our hearts.

Fourth, to those who view intuition as a mysterious force, out of reach for the practical-minded—think again! Intuition, like any skill, can be developed, sharpened, and mastered with techniques such as meditation, mindfulness, and journaling, deepening our connection with this inner sanctuary.

By dispelling these myths, we step into our role as empowered women, seekers, entrepreneurs, and trailblazers. "Awaken Your Intuition" is more than just a book; it is a guide, leading us to harness our intuitive talents with elegance and assurance. With a blend of practical exercises, transformative stories, and wise counsel, we are equipped to awaken our intuition, revolutionizing both our personal paths and professional pursuits.

So, let us cast aside those superstitions, have faith in our profound inner knowledge, and start this life-changing journey toward an existence rich with intuition, achievement, and serenity. Embrace your intuition, and watch as doors to new opportunities swing open, propelling you toward greater heights of success and inner harmony.

## *The Connection between Intuition and Success*

Success is often measured by tangible achievements and milestones, yet there's a less visible, but incredibly powerful, force at play—our intuition. Known as our "sixth sense," this inner guidance helps navigate us through choices, obstacles, and opportunities. This section encourages us to delve into how embracing our intuitive insights can bring about significant changes for women in all spheres of life and business.

For women, intuition is more than a mere talent; it is a legacy and a vital connection to the inner wisdom we all possess. However, in a world dominated by rational thought, many of us have learned to doubt or suppress this crucial voice. "Awaken Your Intuition" serves as a rallying cry to break away from these constraints, inviting us to rediscover and honor our intuitive nature.

By choosing to trust and follow our intuition, we find that the universe aligns with our aspirations. Whether unraveling complex decisions or fueling our creative sparks, intuition acts as our guiding light, unveiling routes and insights that align with our true desires and aspirations.

In the dynamic realm of business and innovation, intuition is our invaluable asset. It steers astute entrepreneurs toward critical decisions, identifies emerging trends, and helps build meaningful partnerships that align with their goals. For women in the workforce, honing this intuitive acumen can be the key to shifting from being followers to leaders.

Yet, the influence of intuition extends beyond professional success. It is fundamental to personal growth, enabling us to connect with our genuine selves and cultivate enriching relationships.

"Awaken Your Intuition" transcends the ordinary, offering a comprehensive toolkit for personal change, filled with practical exercises, meditations, and narratives designed to kindle and enhance our intuitive spark.

Whether you are seeking deeper self-knowledge, entrepreneurial success, true love and community, or career advancement, let this section be your roadmap. Harness the transformative potential of intuition and embark on a path to a life and career that not only achieves but resonates deeply with your personal truth.

# Chapter 1 Quest

*Intuitive Journaling Exercise: Meet Your Inner Guide*

## Objective

To create a deeper connection with your intuition and to learn to recognize its voice among the many thoughts and feelings that you experience daily.

## Materials Needed

A journal or notebook

A quiet, comfortable space

An open mind and heart

## Instructions

Set the Scene: Find a quiet space where you will not be disturbed. Make it comfortable and inviting, perhaps lighting a candle or incense to create a serene atmosphere.

Ground Yourself: Begin with a few minutes of deep breathing or a short meditation to center yourself. Envision grounding energy flowing through your body, connecting you to the earth, and creating a space of openness and receptivity.

Intention Setting: Write down your intention for this exercise at the top of your page. It could be as simple as, "My intention is to connect with and understand my intuitive voice more clearly."

The Dialogue Begins: Start by writing a question to your intuition about a decision or situation in your life that you need guidance on. Phrase it in a way that feels open-ended and not leading towards a specific answer.

Listen and Write: Pause for a moment, clearing your mind and waiting for a response. This might come as a feeling, word, image, or sensation. Trust whatever comes up and begin writing. Do not judge or analyze; just let the words flow onto the page.

Deepen the Conversation: Continue the dialogue by asking more questions, seeking clarity or further insight into the initial guidance you received. Remember, this conversation is with your deepest self, so be open, curious, and accepting of whatever arises.

Reflect and Plan: After you feel the dialogue has reached a natural conclusion, spend some time reflecting on the experience. What did you learn about your intuition and how it communicates with you? How can you apply this guidance to your life or business?

**Gratitude and Closing**

Finish the exercise by expressing gratitude to your intuition for the guidance provided. Acknowledge the effort and intention you have put into this exercise. Close your session with a few deep, grounding breaths, bringing the energy of the exercise into your daily life.

## Integration

Make intuitive journaling a regular practice, experimenting with different questions and scenarios. Notice how your ability to connect with and understand your intuition evolves over time. Consider integrating insights from this practice into your decision-making processes, both in personal and professional contexts.

This exercise aims to demystify the process of engaging with your intuition, encouraging a proactive and interactive approach to understanding and utilizing this powerful inner resource. Through regular practice, you can enhance your intuitive clarity, confidence, and the ability to incorporate intuition into your journey toward success in life and business.

*Chapter 2*

# DEVELOPING YOUR INTUITIVE ABILITIES

### *Expanding Awareness*

"Expanding Awareness" invites us on a profound journey to connect deeply with our inner strength and wisdom. As women, whether we are pioneering in the business world, spearheading careers, or embarking on living our truth, life presents a symphony of unique rhythms and challenges. This chapter delves into the transformative practice of attuning ourselves to our intuitive voice, enabling us to traverse life's complexities with grace and profound understanding.

Embarking on the journey of heightened awareness begins with the essential practice of inward listening. We explore a variety of techniques and exercises specifically crafted to quiet the noise of the external world, thus allowing us to tune into the subtle whispers of our soul. By grounding ourselves in the moment, we discover the rich guidance residing within us. This chapter unfolds as a comprehensive guide filled with actionable wisdom to strengthen our intuitive bond, fostering significant personal growth and a deeper sense of self-awareness.

Further, expanding our awareness entails a vigilant observation of our thoughts, emotions, and behaviors. It is about identifying and releasing the burdens of limiting beliefs and habits that obscure our inner brilliance. We are provided with effective strategies to emancipate ourselves, embracing our full potential with open arms.

In the realm of business, a honed intuition shines brightly, guiding us in decision-making, nurturing authentic connections, and uncovering paths that resonate with our truest values and aspirations. This chapter thoughtfully addresses the specific challenges and opportunities encountered in professional settings, offering insights of intuitive wisdom to steer us towards success.

"Expanding Awareness" serves as an invitation for women prepared to awaken their intuitive senses and claim their inner strength. It is a journey through life armed with clarity, making decisions grounded in a deep sense of knowing, and attaining success that aligns with our soul's purpose. This chapter stands as an empowering guide for every seeker, entrepreneur, and professional on their path towards self-discovery and empowerment.

## *Embracing Your Inner Guidance*

The extraordinary power of our intuition, that internal compass and authentic voice of our soul, is indeed one of our greatest treasures. "Awaken Your Intuition: Empowering Women for Success in Life and Business" offers a deep dive into the sacred practice of embracing our inner guidance, demonstrating how this trust can uplift women in every aspect of their lives.

For women charting their courses through the diverse terrains of personal and professional life, intuition is not merely beneficial; it is transformative. It provides clarity, confidence, and a guiding light, empowering us to make bold decisions that align with our essence and navigate life with authenticity and intent. This chapter extends a heartfelt invitation to forge a deep connection with and reliance on our intuition, laying a solid foundation for success in all our endeavors.

Particularly for entrepreneurs and those focused on their careers, intuition emerges as an invaluable companion. In the fast-paced world of business, where decisions demand swift, decisive action, turning to our instinctual understanding can be our most trustworthy guide. We delve into methods for refining this intuitive sense, including meditation, mindfulness, journaling, and self-reflection, offering tools to cultivate a profound relationship with our inner wisdom.

Additionally, we address the shadows of doubt and fear that may obscure our confidence in our intuitive abilities. By redefining intuition as a sophisticated form of intelligence and sharing stories of women who have achieved success by following their instincts, we dismantle any notion that intuition is anything but a formidable ally.

"Embracing Your Inner Guidance" is not merely a chapter; it is a rallying cry for women, seekers, entrepreneurs, and visionaries, urging them to leverage the transformative power of intuition. By engaging with this inner source of knowledge, we empower ourselves to make choices that not only overcome challenges but also chart a course to personal and professional success. With detailed guidance and inspiring narratives, these chapters acts as your mentor in awakening your intuition and realizing your utmost potential.

## Mastering Intuitive Decision-Making

As women, whether we are explorers of truth, innovators in business, or leaders in our fields, we frequently find ourselves in pivotal roles, making decisions that sculpt our lives and careers. Herein lies the enchantment of intuition, our internal guide, shining as our beacon of light. So many of us our using our intuition all day without realizing that it is working in the background in almost all choices we make.

"Awaken Your Intuition" transcends being merely a book; it is an expedition into embracing that spark of intuitive wisdom for triumph in every facet of our existence. Venturing further into intuitive decision-making, we discover techniques to fine-tune this innate capability. Envision quieting the cacophony of the outside world to hear the gentle whispers of your soul through practices like meditation, journaling, or moments of quiet introspection. It is about crafting a haven for your intuition to flourish.

Believing in ourselves is the foundation of living intuitively. This chapter inspires us to trust our inner wisdom, standing firm against the barrage of external judgments. Through affirmations and mindful practices, we strengthen our trust in our intuitive voice, differentiating it from the fears and doubts that may mislead us.

Throughout this book we will introduce a range of daily practices for engaging intuitively—from visualization and intuitive writing to conversations with our deeper self. These practices serve as our allies in ensuring our decisions are aligned with our core beliefs and goals.

Adopting intuitive decision-making unlocks a treasure within, steering us with assurance and clarity. This journey invites us to place our trust in our intuition, leading to a life and career imbued with authenticity and success. Embark on this transformative adventure, awakening to the prosperity and satisfaction that comes from intuitive living and the gift of hearing your still small voice of truth within.

# Chapter 2 Quest

## *Exercise: Letter from Your Intuition*

Writing a letter to yourself from the perspective of your intuition is a powerful exercise to foster trust and deepen your connection with your inner guidance. Here is a step-by-step guide to help you embark on this reflective and transformative journey:

### Objective

To cultivate a trusting relationship with your intuition by allowing it to communicate directly with you, offering insights, reassurance, and guidance.

### Preparation

Find a quiet, comfortable space where you can reflect without interruptions.

Choose a medium for writing that feels most natural to you, whether it is pen and paper, a journal, or a digital document.

Take a few deep breaths to center yourself and set the intention to be open and receptive to the wisdom your intuition has to offer.

**Writing the Letter**

Greeting: Begin your letter with a warm, personal greeting. This letter is from a place of love and wisdom within you, so address yourself in a way that feels nurturing.

Acknowledgment: Have your intuition acknowledge your efforts, struggles, and the journey you have been on. This is an opportunity for your intuition to recognize where you have shown strength, resilience, and growth.

Insights: Allow your intuition to offer insights into current situations or decisions you are facing. This is not about providing clear-cut answers but rather offering a perspective that you may not have considered, highlighting your inner knowledge and wisdom.

Reassurance: Let your intuition reassure you about the fears and doubts you hold. This could involve affirming that you have the strength to face challenges or reminding you that you are not alone, even when you feel most isolated.

Guidance: Ask your intuition to provide guidance on how to more effectively listen and connect with it in your daily life. This might include suggestions for practices, signs to watch for, or affirmations to repeat.

Closing: Conclude your letter with words of encouragement and love. Have your intuition remind you of your inherent worth, the beauty of your journey, and the bright path ahead.

## Reflection

After writing your letter, take some time to reflect on the experience. Consider these questions:

How did it feel to write this letter? Was it challenging, comforting, enlightening?

Were there any surprises or new insights that emerged?

How can you incorporate the guidance from this letter into your daily life?

## Integration

Keep the letter somewhere safe and accessible. Return to it whenever you need a reminder of your intuition's presence and wisdom. You may also want to create a ritual of writing a new letter at regular intervals (e.g., every new year, on your birthday, or during significant life transitions) to keep the dialogue with your intuition active and evolving.

This exercise is designed to be a heart-opening dialogue with the deepest, wisest part of yourself. It is a reminder that your intuition is a loving ally on your journey, always ready to guide, support, and uplift you.

*Chapter 3*

# CLEARING
# BLOCKS TO
# INTUITION

### *Transcending Doubt and Fear*

As we journey through the complex landscapes of life and aspiration, it is not uncommon to find ourselves confronting the formidable shadows of doubt and fear. These emotional barriers, ever-present on the periphery of our consciousness, can significantly hinder the blossoming of our intuitive capabilities. For us women, who are visionaries, pioneers, and trailblazers in our respective fields, recognizing and overcoming these shadows is paramount for unleashing the full spectrum of our intuition's radiant power.

Doubt, with its sly and undermining whispers, often casts a long shadow on our confidence, instilling hesitation and uncertainty within us. However, when we come to perceive doubt not as a reflection of our incapacity but rather as a mirage, born from past experiences and societal expectations, we begin to reclaim control over our narrative.

Fear, although daunting, serves as a signal that we are on the brink of exploring new territories of personal and professional growth. By welcoming fear as an indicator of evolution rather than a force of opposition, we diminish its grip on our actions and decisions. The path to overcoming these emotions is rooted in self-awareness— delving into the origins of these feelings, recognizing the patterns they form in our lives, and understanding how they have shaped our journey thus far.

Imposter syndrome is another concept making the headlines these days that describes a feeling of insecurity in one's abilities. This seems to be especially true of women as we never seem to get the same support of our abilities to succeed when we are coming up as men do. Many of us are terrified that the lives we have created for ourselves are going to come crashing down due to some character flaw deep within us. Even Oprah Winfrey has fears of becoming a bag lady and has questioned her own abilities. This same imposter syndrome doubles down when it comes to us trusting ourselves.

By surrounding ourselves with a supportive community of like-minded individuals, who offer upliftment and guidance, we can dramatically transform our experience and help ourselves develop trust in ourselves and others. Add to that the transformative practices of positive affirmations, visualization, and mindfulness, and we begin to reshape our mindset, celebrating every step forward, no matter its size, and strengthening our belief in the path we have chosen.

Embracing patience, perseverance, and self-compassion becomes crucial as we navigate this journey. By placing our trust in the intuitive wisdom that resides within us, we tap into an inexhaustible well of knowledge and strength, propelling us toward the realization of our dreams in both life and our professional endeavors.

## *Liberating Ourselves from Limiting Beliefs*

In our pursuit of personal and professional excellence, we often encounter internal roadblocks in the form of deeply ingrained beliefs that we just aren't worthy. These beliefs, whether they stem from early life experiences, societal narratives, or past failures, can create formidable barriers that prevent us from fully embracing the power of our intuition.

Intuition is an invaluable asset, particularly for us women. It acts as our unseen guide, fueling our creativity, informing our decisions, and helping us navigate through the complexities of life. However, the weight of limiting beliefs—such as the fear of failure, the illusion of success scarcity, and feelings of unworthiness—can obscure the light of our intuitive guidance.

By confronting the fear of failure and recognizing every misstep as an integral part of our growth journey, we start to view challenges in a new light. Adopting an abundance mindset allows us to see success as an expansive, limitless realm, open to all who dare to dream. And, as we begin to dissolve the doubts surrounding our worth, we stand confidently in our power, acknowledging our rightful place in the world of achievement and aspiration.

Embarking on a transformative journey through mindfulness, meditation, journaling, and the use of affirmations, we actively replace outdated narratives with empowering truths that resonate with our innermost selves. As we shed these limiting beliefs, we allow our intuition to soar, guiding us toward a future filled with unlimited potential.

This sacred journey of awakening our intuition is, at its core, an act of self-empowerment. It invites us to step fully into our light, embracing the success and fulfillment our hearts deeply desire.

## *Healing Emotional Traumas*

In the pursuit of self-discovery and growth, addressing and healing our emotional wounds is an indispensable step. These wounds, often the result of past hurts, traumas, or negative experiences, can anchor us, hindering our ability to reach our full potential. This chapter delves into the crucial process of healing these emotional scars, highlighting its importance for women, seekers, entrepreneurs, and professionals alike, and underscoring its synergy with the journey to awaken our intuition.

Emotional wounds can manifest in various ways, including as persistent self-doubt, fear of failure, or difficulties in forming meaningful relationships. Yet, it is through confronting and healing these wounds that we embark on a path of profound personal empowerment and transformation.

For women, the act of healing is especially significant. Societal pressures and expectations often place undue burdens on us, but through the process of healing, we can reclaim our true selves, celebrating our unique strengths and pursuing our dreams with renewed vigor and passion. Seekers on spiritual quests will find that addressing emotional baggage sheds light on the path to deeper self-awareness and spiritual enlightenment.

In the professional realm, entrepreneurs and career-oriented women face their own unique challenges, from navigating past failures to combating imposter syndrome. Healing these emotional injuries not only frees their intuition and creative spirit but also strengthens their decision-making abilities, setting the stage for unparalleled success.

"Awaken Your Intuition" underscores the pivotal role of intuition in our lives. By healing our past pains, we clear the fog from our intuitive lens, allowing us to move forward with clarity and purpose in every aspect of our lives. In order to really be able to receive the messages of insight and guidance, we need to make a space for them to come through and that often requires working on the old wounds that often stand in our way.

The work of this chapter is to encourage you to embark on your own healing adventure to be the best that you can be. By arming women, seekers, and leaders with the necessary tools for their healing journey, we unlock the door to boundless potential, fostering a deep sense of self-love and understanding that enables us to live the empowered lives for which we are destined.

# Chapter 3 Quest

## *Emotional Healing Modalities*

Emotional healing modalities are diverse, reflecting the wide range of human experiences and the unique ways individuals process their emotions. Here is a list of various emotional healing modalities, each offering its own approach to fostering emotional well-being:

Counseling or Psychotherapy: Talk therapy with a trained therapist can help individuals understand and work through emotional issues, traumas, and mental health disorders.

Cognitive Behavioral Therapy (CBT): A structured, time-limited therapy that aims to change patterns of thinking or behavior that are behind people's difficulties, and so change the way they feel.

Eye Movement Desensitization and Reprocessing (EMDR): A psychotherapy treatment designed to alleviate the distress associated with traumatic memories.

Mindfulness-Based Stress Reduction (MBSR): A program that uses mindfulness meditation to help people manage stress, anxiety, depression, and pain.

Emotionally Focused Therapy (EFT): A structured approach to couples therapy formulated in the 1980s that focuses on adult relationships and attachment/bonding.

Art Therapy: A form of expressive therapy that uses the creative process of making art to improve a person's physical, mental, and emotional well-being.

Music Therapy: The use of music to address emotional, cognitive, and social needs of individuals.

Dance/Movement Therapy: A therapeutic form of exercise that promotes emotional, social, cognitive, and physical integration of the individual.

Yoga and Meditation: Practices that combine physical postures, breathing exercises, meditation, and ethical precepts to enhance well-being.

Reiki and Energy Healing: Techniques that involve the transfer of energy from practitioner to patient to enhance the body's natural ability to heal itself through the balancing of energy.

Breathwork: A range of breathing techniques used to improve mental, physical, and spiritual well-being.

Narrative Therapy: An approach to therapy that centers people as the experts in their own lives and uses stories to shape people's understanding of their lives and problems.

Acupuncture: A component of traditional Chinese medicine that is used to treat pain and is increasingly being used for overall wellness, including stress management.

Herbal Medicine and Aromatherapy: The use of plant-based remedies and essential oils to improve emotional and physical health.

Biofeedback: A technique that teaches individuals how to control bodily processes that are normally involuntary, such as muscle tension, blood pressure, or heart rate, to improve health and performance.

Animal-Assisted Therapy: The use of animals, such as dogs or horses, to help individuals recover from or better cope with health problems, including emotional and mental health issues.

Spiritual Counseling: Guidance and support on spiritual matters, often integrating principles from various spiritual traditions to help individuals find purpose, connection, and inner peace.

Hypnotherapy: The use of hypnosis as a therapeutic technique to access the subconscious mind and introduce positive changes in perceptions, sensations, emotions, thoughts, or behavior.

Crystal Healing: The use of crystals and gemstones to promote physical and emotional healing by influencing the body's energy fields.

Shamanic Healing: Ancient healing practices involving journeys to other worlds or dimensions to obtain healing and guidance from spirits, ancestors, and other beings.

Each of these modalities offers unique benefits and may resonate differently with each individual depending on their personal experiences, beliefs, and needs. It is often beneficial to explore multiple approaches to find the ones that best support one's journey toward emotional health and well-being. I highly encourage determining what areas of your life need a little dose of TLC so you can do self care. There is no shame in admitting when we need help and allowing ourselves to benefit from the array of assistance that is out there. It is amazing how quickly we grow through challenges when intuition is assisting our journey.

*Chapter 4*

# INTUITION IN PERSONAL RELATIONSHIPS

## *Deepening Friendships Through Intuitive Understanding*

Friendships, those invaluable treasures of life, provide us with warmth, companionship, and a profound sense of belonging. "Deepening Friendships Through Intuitive Understanding," a compelling chapter from "Awaken Your Intuition: Empowering Women for Success in Life and Business," asks us to harness our intuitive gifts to enrich and deepen these vital connections. Our intuition, that urging from within, serves as our compass, enabling us to forge more authentic connections and discern the true nature and intentions of those we consider friends. Amidst a society that often esteems rational thought above emotional insight, this chapter stands as a testament to the extraordinary experiences that unfold when we allow our intuition to guide our friendships.

This exploration delves into the ways in which intuitive bonds cultivate authenticity, provide emotional support, and foster personal growth. Through engaging in meditation, journaling, and sincere reflection, we quiet the external distractions to listen to our heart's wisdom. This path also educates us in the fine arts of deep listening and empathetic communication, thus enriching our understanding and strengthening our connections with friends in our circle.

Furthermore, we can learn and honor the importance of setting intuitive boundaries to nurture friendships that uplift us and resonate with our highest selves while gracefully managing those that do not. This chapter presents practices and insights aimed at nurturing friendships and other relationships that reflect our innermost values and support our growth, both personally and professionally.

## Harnessing Intuition in Romantic Endeavors

The complex ballet of romantic relationships often requires guidance, and our intuition shines brightly as a beacon, leading us towards connections that resonate with our spirit and helping us navigate potential heartaches. In a realm saturated with external pressures and societal norms, turning to our inner voice in matters of the heart may appear challenging. Yet, for us—women empowered with insight, ambition, and depth—fostering our intuitive sense is crucial for building relationships that echo our deepest realities.

Embarking on a self-discovery voyage illuminates the signals our intuition sends, equipping us to move through the romantic domain with elegance and awareness. Distinguishing the true call of our intuition from the tumult of fear is essential, as is finding moments of stillness amidst life's chaos through practices like meditation, mindfulness, and self-reflection. This journey towards intuitive alignment requires patience, self-kindness, and a dedication to learning, forming the bedrock for crafting love stories imbued with authenticity and happiness.

To welcome our intuition in love is to begin a quest for relationships that are both profound and sincere. It entails a consistent practice of self-examination, the discernment between genuine intuitive insights and fear-based reactions, the pursuit of peace in our bustling existences, and a wholehearted commitment to this transformative exploration. Through this process, we open our hearts to the immense possibilities of love that seamlessly aligns with our essence, weaving a narrative of romance that is not only fulfilling but also deeply harmonious.

## Fortifying Family Ties with Intuitive Insight

Perhaps one of the most acceptable forms of extra sensitive perception is " Mother's Intuition" For us dynamic women juggling the demands of entrepreneurship, career progression and personal quests, the task of sustaining and enhancing our family relationships can appear formidable but one that society places on us to handle as the emotional center of our families. However, nestled within us is a potent, natural tool—our intuition that we women seem to come equipped with. This profound inner guidance, a voice of wisdom that transcends the confines of logic, is the key to strengthening our familial bonds. It is about transcending mere understanding to deeply resonate with their aspirations, unvoiced feelings, and desires, thereby creating an environment rich in empathy, support, and unconditional love.

Awakening our intuition allows us to become more attuned to the silent languages spoken by our family members, enhancing our interactions and turning each moment into an opportunity for collective growth and deeper connection. Our intuition acts as our navigator through the complexities of family life, from resolving tensions with grace to making significant decisions with assurance.

"Awaken Your Intuition: Empowering Women for Success in Life and Business" not only recognizes this invaluable gift but also offers tangible steps to activate it within the sphere of family dynamics. Through meditation, introspection, and a selection of intuition-boosting activities, we are encouraged to look inward, fortifying our connection to our intuitive selves. This guide promises not just an awakening of our intuitive faculties but a transformation of our family life into a sanctuary of deeper understanding, mutual respect, and harmonious co-living.

By embracing our intuitive power, we lay the foundation for a family life filled with love, comprehension, and a collective journey towards fulfillment. As women we are thrust into the roles of being an emotional compass because we are, by virtue of our intuition, best equipped for it. Let us commit to using our gifts to help connect with, guide and inspire all of those in our life sphere and step into our power to lead with love in our rich tapestry of personal connections.

# Chapter 4 Quests

## *Intuitive Friendship Circle*

This activity aims to create a supportive space where friends can deepen their connections through the power of intuition. Below are detailed guidelines to facilitate a meaningful and transformative experience:

### Preparation

Choosing a Setting: Select a quiet, comfortable space conducive to openness and relaxation. This could be someone's living room, a private garden, or any place where the group feels safe and undisturbed.

Setting the Ambiance: Consider setting up the space with comfortable seating arranged in a circle. You might add elements such as candles, soft lighting, or soothing background music to create a calm and inviting atmosphere.

Communicating the Purpose: Before gathering, explain the objective of the Intuitive Friendship Circle to your friends. Emphasize the importance of confidentiality, respect, and non-judgment to create a trustworthy environment.

**Activity Steps**

**Opening Meditation**

Duration: Aim for a 5-10 minute meditation to ensure everyone is centered and ready.

Guidance: You can lead the meditation yourself, focusing on deep breathing and visualization techniques to help everyone connect with their inner voice, or use a guided meditation from a trusted source.

Intention Setting: Encourage participants to set personal intentions for openness, empathy, and connection.

**Sharing Personal Challenges**

Moderation: As the facilitator, gently guide the sharing process to ensure each person has time to speak without interruptions.

Brevity and Focus: Remind everyone to keep their shares concise, focusing on the essence of their challenge or question to leave room for intuitive responses.

**Offering Intuitive Feedback**

Speaking from the Heart: Encourage participants to share their initial thoughts, feelings, or images that come to mind, emphasizing the importance of kindness and positive intentions.

Respecting Boundaries: Remind the group that feedback should be offered from a place of support and not as direct advice or criticism.

## Discussion and Reflection

Sharing Resonance: After each round of sharing and feedback, allow the original speaker to express how the intuitive insights resonated with them. This can lead to deeper insights and shared experiences.

Group Reflection: Conclude each sharing cycle with a brief moment for the group to reflect on the process and share any collective insights or feelings about the experience.

## Closing the Circle

Gratitude Sharing: Finish the session by going around the circle, with each person sharing something they are grateful for from the experience.

Closing Meditation or Ritual: Consider ending with a short meditation or a simple ritual, such as a group hug or a moment of silence, to seal the shared experience and gently transition back to everyday consciousness.

Feedback and Sharing: After the session, encourage informal feedback or sharing about how the experience impacted them or any subsequent reflections.

## Tips for Success

Lead with Vulnerability: As the facilitator, sharing your own experiences or challenges vulnerably can set the tone for others to do the same.

Create a Safe Space: Continuously reinforce the importance of confidentiality and non-judgment to maintain a safe and supportive environment.

Be Flexible: Allow the activity to flow naturally. Be open to adjusting the structure based on the group's needs and dynamics.

The Intuitive Friendship Circle is designed not only to deepen connections but also to provide a unique space for personal growth and mutual support. Through this exercise, friends can explore the profound impact of intuitive understanding and empathy in their relationships.

## Exercise: The Intuitive Love Letter

**Objective**: To connect with your intuition about love, relationships, and what you truly desire in a partner.

**Materials Needed:**

- A quiet, comfortable space
- Journal or paper
- Pen
- Candle (optional, for creating a serene atmosphere)

**Steps**

**Preparation**: Find a quiet space where you feel comfortable and at ease. If you like, light a candle to create a serene atmosphere. Sit comfortably and take a few deep breaths. Close your eyes and focus on your breathing, allowing yourself to become more relaxed with each breath.

**Grounding**: With your eyes closed, visualize roots extending from your body deep into the earth. Imagine these roots grounding you and connecting you to the earth's energy. Feel this connection stabilize and center you, providing a foundation for your intuitive exploration.

**Heart Centering**: Place your hands over your heart. Envision a warm, glowing light in your heart space, growing brighter and more radiant with each breath. This light represents your love, your essence, and your capacity for connection. Sit with this feeling, allowing it to fill you with warmth and peace.

**The Intuitive Love Letter**: Open your eyes and turn to your journal or paper. Write a letter to your future self or a future partner, but let this be guided purely by your intuition. Start with "Dear [Your Name/Future Love]," and let the words flow without judgment. Write about what love means to you, what you wish for in love, and how you see yourself in a loving relationship. Do not worry about grammar or coherence; focus on expressing your true feelings and desires.

**Reflection**: After you have finished writing, read your letter. Reflect on the emotions, desires, and insights that emerged. What surprised you? What feels most true? Take a moment to sit with these reflections, acknowledging your intuition's role in guiding you toward what your heart truly seeks in love.

**Closing**: Thank your intuition for the guidance provided. Envision sending love and gratitude to your future self or partner. Close the exercise with a few deep breaths, feeling grounded and connected to your heart's wisdom.

**Integration**

This exercise is not just about the act of writing but about integrating these insights into your daily life. Reflect on your letter in the coming days. Consider what actions you can take or changes you can make to align more closely with your intuitive insights about love. Remember, intuition is a powerful guide, especially when it comes to matters of the heart. Trust in it, and let it lead you towards the love you desire and deserve.

## Chapter 5

# INTUITION IN PROFESSIONAL LIFE

### *Empowering Professional Dynamics Through Intuitive Insight*

In the modern professional landscape, women are increasingly celebrated for their leadership acumen and innovative capabilities, with many attributing their achievements to a resource often sidelined: intuition. This insightful chapter from "Awaken Your Intuition: Empowering Women for Success in Life and Business" shines a light on the strategic application of intuition within the workplace. It reveals the transformative influence of intuitive perception in enhancing decision-making processes, sparking innovation, and fostering meaningful professional relationships, positioning intuition not as an elusive gift but as a tangible skill that can be refined and purposefully integrated into professional practices.

The journey towards harnessing one's intuitive prowess begins with the cultivation of self-awareness. By embarking on a path of self-discovery, women can fine-tune their ability to distinguish the nuanced whispers of intuition from the cacophony of daily thoughts and emotional turbulence. This endeavor involves immersing oneself in introspective practices, such as meditation or journaling, facilitating a journey towards deeper comprehension and confidence in one's intuitive insights. The narrative champions self-awareness not merely as a journey towards self-knowledge but as a strategic approach to augmenting professional intuition.

Further, the chapter supports the indispensable role of intuition in making complex decisions within the professional domain. We will discuss how intuitive judgment can complement analytical reasoning to produce holistic and impactful solutions. This synergistic approach empowers women to confront their career challenges with a balanced perspective, ensuring their decisions are both logically sound and deeply resonant with their core values and aspirations.

Additionally, the importance of fostering a work environment that celebrates intuitive insight is underscored as crucial for both individual and collective advancement within organizations. The chapter presents ways that you can begin cultivating confidence in your own intuitive capabilities to help foster a workplace ethos that not only acknowledges but actively champions the expression of intuitive wisdom. By promoting an atmosphere where intuition is acknowledged as a legitimate and influential force, women are encouraged to more freely engage this inner resource, leading to enriched career trajectories and significant contributions to their fields.

## Innovating Through Intuitive Business Insights

Today's business world is a roller coaster of pressure and stress and the art of making astute and effective decisions is paramount to success. However, an exclusive reliance on logical analysis may not always capture the full spectrum of potential outcomes and can dampen the creative and visionary spark. More and more, intuition is emerging as a formidable ally in this context, guiding strategic decisions and propelling women towards professional achievement. This section underscores the critical importance of intuitive decision-making, showcasing the profound impact intuition can have in empowering women on their professional journeys.

Intuition, often experienced as an instinctual gut feeling or a profound hunch, represents our innermost wisdom, providing clarity in moments of uncertainty or complexity. Women, with their intrinsic emotional intelligence and empathic capacities, are uniquely positioned to harness their intuitive insights. Whether as entrepreneurs, career-driven professionals, or individuals in pursuit of personal fulfillment, women stand to benefit from embracing their intuitive strengths. By welcoming intuition, they unlock deeper insights and perspectives that transcend conventional rational analysis.

To cultivate a strong intuitive sense, it is essential to allocate time for self-reflection and mindfulness, achievable through meditation, journaling, and other mindfulness practices. I know I am repetitive here but these practices cannot be stressed often enough. Silencing the external noise to connect with our inner guidance allows us to recognize and act upon our intuitive impulses—be it a persistent thought, a spontaneous feeling, or an unshakable conviction—thus unveiling opportunities and pathways that might otherwise remain hidden.

Delving into the experiences of successful women we find those who have successfully integrated intuition into their business strategies offers both inspiration and practical guidance for weaving intuition into everyday professional decisions. By awakening our intuitive faculties, women in the business realm can navigate challenges with greater insight, embrace opportunities with confidence, and realize their full potential in the competitive business landscape.

## *Cultivating Intuitive Leadership Qualities*

The essence of effective leadership today goes beyond conventional logic to embrace a dimension often overlooked: intuition. This inner guidance system serves as a luminary, guiding us towards judicious decisions and fostering connections that resonate on a profound level. In this dedicated exploration, we unveil the process of developing intuitive leadership skills, illuminating how this approach can elevate women to new heights in both their personal and professional lives.

Adopting intuitive leadership involves tuning in to our inner wisdom, allowing our instinctual feelings to inform our leadership decisions. It is about acknowledging the value of our internal voice and integrating its insights into our decision-making processes. This journey enriches our self-understanding, enhances our ability to empathize with others, and equips us to navigate situations with innovative perspectives. Intuitive leaders adeptly manage the ebb and flow of change and uncertainty, their heightened senses attuned to embracing novel directions and solutions.

For women, fostering intuitive leadership skills offers a distinctive form of empowerment. Our natural propensity towards intuition, when finely honed, infuses leadership with grace, empathy, and warmth, creating a workplace that thrives on inclusivity and mutual respect.

As we delve into this exploration, we discover methods for awakening and refining our intuitive leadership abilities. We emphasize the importance of self-reflection, mindfulness, and meditation as key practices for enhancing our intuitive awareness. Additionally, we examine how emotional intelligence amplifies our ability to connect deeply with others and make enlightened leadership choices.

Progressing further, we will explore intuition's role within entrepreneurial endeavors and career development. We will provide real world case studies that highlight how our instincts in business undertakings, navigating critical decisions, and seizing opportunities with vigor can transform our lives for the better. Through breakdowns of real world examples of intuition in action we showcase the dynamic power of intuitive leadership in fostering personal growth and professional success.

Whether you are an aspiring entrepreneur, a seasoned business professional, or someone climbing the career ladder, embarking on the path to intuitive leadership offers a journey filled with discovery and empowerment. By blending intuition with traditional leadership models, you unlock a reservoir of potential, stepping into a leadership role that not only inspires but also transforms and rewards you and those around you with honest and meaningful connection.

# Chapter 5 Quest

## *Ways To Incorporate Intuition In Your Career Role Now*

Intuition in the business world is often referred to as 'gut feeling', and it can be a crucial tool for making decisions, fostering innovation, and navigating complex interpersonal dynamics. Here are ten ways you can harness your intuition to enhance your business acumen and leadership:

### Decision Making

Trust Your Gut: When faced with difficult decisions, after gathering and analyzing all the data, allow your gut feeling to have a say. Often, your subconscious mind can process information in ways your conscious mind cannot, leading to insights that are not immediately obvious.

### Reading People

Sensing Motives and Feelings: Use your intuition to sense the motives and feelings of colleagues, clients, and business partners. This can help you navigate negotiations, partnerships, and team dynamics more effectively, by understanding what drives the people you are dealing with.

## Hiring Talent

Identifying Cultural Fit: Beyond evaluating skills and experience, use your intuition to gauge whether a candidate will be a good cultural fit for your team. Sometimes, a candidate's energy or vibe can indicate how well they will integrate and collaborate with your existing team.

## Predicting Trends

Anticipating Market Movements: Intuition can play a role in sensing shifts in consumer behavior or emerging industry trends before they become obvious. This foresight can be invaluable in positioning your business to capitalize on new opportunities.

## Managing Risks

Sensing Warning Signs: Intuition can help you pick up on subtle warning signs that a project or investment might not be going as well as reported. This can prompt further investigation and potentially save your company from making costly mistakes.

## Innovation and Creativity

Inspiration for New Ideas: Sometimes, innovative ideas come from a place beyond logical reasoning. Allowing your intuition to guide your creative process can lead to unique solutions and breakthrough products or services.

## Conflict Resolution

Understanding Underlying Issues**: In conflicts, intuition can help you read between the lines and understand the real issues at play, which might not be openly discussed. This deeper understanding can lead to more effective and lasting resolutions.

## Strategic Planning

Guidance on Long-Term Vision: When planning for the future, intuition can help you envision where you want your business to go and what it can become. It can guide you in setting long-term goals that align with your core values and vision.

## Customer Relations

Empathizing with Clients: Use your intuition to better understand and empathize with your clients' needs and concerns, even when they might not be able to articulate them clearly. This can strengthen client relationships and improve customer satisfaction.

## Personal Well-being

Balancing Work and Life: Intuition can signal when you are pushing too hard or risking burnout. Listening to these internal cues can help you maintain a healthier balance between work and personal life, ensuring you remain productive and motivated.

Incorporating intuition into your business practices requires openness, self-awareness, and the courage to sometimes go against conventional wisdom. Cultivating your intuitive abilities can provide you with a nuanced and comprehensive approach to business leadership and decision-making.

## Chapter 6

# INTUITION AND ENTREPRENEURSHIP

### *Harnessing Intuition for Uncovering Business Ventures*

Today's professional landscape with the market oversaturation and cut throat competition you really need a super power to stand out from the crowd and prosper. Beyond the traditional methods of market analysis, data interpretation, and strategic planning, lies a path less traveled yet brimming with potential—intuition. Embracing this inner compass provides a unique advantage in recognizing and developing valuable opportunities that others might overlook.

Intuition, our innate "sixth sense," is a natural gift we all possess. It is that immediate gut feeling, that flash of insight that leaps ahead of rational thought. For women, renowned for their stereotypical strong intuitive sense, tapping into this inner wisdom can be a game-changer, significantly tipping the scales in favor of both personal growth and entrepreneurial success.

This chapter shines a light on utilizing intuition to discover business opportunities. It encourages women to dive deep into their intuitive abilities, guiding them to use it as a beacon in uncharted territories. By tuning into the subtle hints, signs, and gentle nudges intuition provides, women can make decisions and take risks with a mix of foresight and boldness.

We begin by clarifying that intuition is not some esoteric, unreliable phenomenon. Drawing from scientific research and real-world success stories, the significance of intuition in business is made clear. It is emphasized that intuition does not replace logic or analytical thinking but rather complements them, enriching the decision-making process.

Later we will transitions to practical methods and exercises aimed at enhancing intuitive senses. Techniques like mindfulness, meditation, and introspection are highlighted, as always, as keys to unlocking intuitive insights. We also stress the importance of honing intuition through active listening, being attuned to bodily signals, and trusting the instincts that spontaneously arise. Paying full attention to yourself, others and your surrounds is imperative in developing intuition.

Furthermore, this chapter explores how intuitive insights can be applied across various business activities—from identifying emerging market trends and understanding customer needs to evaluating potential collaborations or marketing.

For the experienced entrepreneur, the career woman seeking new ventures, or anyone on a journey of self-discovery, this chapter is an invitation to awaken and leverage your intuitive powers. By integrating intuition into your business strategies, you can create a distinctive edge, make more informed decisions, and weave success into the fabric of both your personal and professional life.

## *Integrating Intuition into Marketing Efforts*

Today's commercial climate is a cacophony of information and, in the business world, staying ahead of the curve is essential. While traditional marketing strategies have their place, incorporating intuitive marketing can add a layer of magic, providing that extra sparkle that sets women entrepreneurs and career-focused individuals apart. Intuition, deeply interwoven into the essence of femininity, emerges as a powerful tool when fully embraced that can help you and your efforts get noticed and stand out amongst the fray.

Intuitive marketing involves tapping into your inner wisdom, those gut feelings that offer insights into the hearts and minds of your audience. It is about creating marketing messages that resonate on a deeper level, crafting narratives that not only speak to but also captivate your customers. By integrating intuitive marketing into their arsenal, women can enhance their impact, forge stronger connections with their audience, and pave the way to greater achievements in their businesses and careers.

At the core of intuitive marketing is the practice of listening to your inner voice. Women naturally possess a rich intuition that can guide insightful marketing decisions. Trusting these instincts can reveal customer demographics, desires and drive, predict market trends, and inspire marketing strategies that truly resonate. This intuitive approach breathes authenticity into marketing efforts, making them not just persuasive but genuinely engaging.

Empathy plays a pivotal role in intuitive marketing. Women, known for their empathetic abilities, can unlock a deeper understanding of their audience. By empathizing with customers, they can craft messages that address real needs and aspirations, building a bridge of trust and loyalty that stands the test of time.

Furthermore, intuitive marketing opens the door to creativity and innovation. Women have always been at the forefront of creative thought, and by tapping into this creative wellspring, they can develop marketing strategies that are not only effective but also memorable and impactful.

In conclusion, intuitive marketing holds the key to a realm where women in business can lead with wisdom, empathy, and innovation. By harnessing their innate intuition, understanding, and creative flair, they can create marketing strategies that not only stand out but also deeply connect with their audience. Whether you are an entrepreneur bringing dreams to life, a career woman exploring new frontiers, or a seeker on a path of self-discovery, embracing intuitive marketing lights the way to success in both life and business.

## *Crafting a Flourishing Business with Intuitive Insight*

The journey to a successful intuitive business begins with fostering a profound connection with your intuition. This involves quieting the mind, listening to the soul's whispers, and following the visions it presents. Practices such as meditation significantly enhance your intuitive gifts, unlocking insights and awareness that guide your business decisions.

A key element in building an intuitive business is aligning your actions with your intuitive signals. Learning to perceive and trust these subtle hints and omens can shape your business's essence and direction. This openness to divine guidance ensures that your business moves are not just strategic but also deeply aligned with your authentic self.

Cultivating connections with like-minded individuals—those who share your vision and ideals—enriches your entrepreneurial journey. Surrounding yourself with a supportive community can lead to opportunities, collaborations, and partnerships that elevate your business to new heights.

Moreover, maintaining a mindset of positivity and belief in your intuitive capabilities is crucial. Trusting your inner guidance and recognizing your strengths helps navigate the challenges and uncertainties of entrepreneurship. A resilient and persistent attitude lights your path, enabling you to gracefully maneuver through the ups and downs of business ownership.

Lastly, committing to continuous personal and professional growth is vital for keeping pace with the dynamic business environment.

Engaging in learning opportunities, whether through workshops, courses, or mentorship, enriches both your intuition and business acumen, ensuring your strategies resonate with your target audience's evolving needs.

In summary, weaving a successful intuitive business is a journey of deepening your connection with intuition, making aligned decisions, building supportive relationships, fostering a positive mindset, and embracing lifelong learning. By tapping into the wellspring of intuition, women, seekers, and entrepreneurs can create businesses that not only achieve financial success but also fulfill their deepest aspirations and purposes.

# Chapter 6 Quest

## *Guided Visualization for Connecting with Your Creative Muse*

Welcome to this guided visualization designed to help you connect with your creative muse. Find a quiet, comfortable place where you will not be disturbed. Allow yourself to sit or lie down in a relaxed position. Take a deep breath in, and as you exhale, let go of any tension in your body. Close your eyes and let us embark on a journey to unlock your creative potential.

### Breathing and Relaxing

Start by taking three deep, cleansing breaths. Inhale slowly, filling your lungs with fresh air, and exhale fully, releasing any stress or tension. With each breath, feel more relaxed and open to the creative energy that surrounds you.

### Envisioning Your Sacred Space

Imagine yourself walking on a path through a lush, vibrant forest. With each step, you feel more connected to the earth, more grounded. Notice the sounds of the forest, the chirping of birds, the rustle of leaves underfoot, and the gentle breeze against your skin.

As you walk, you come to a clearing bathed in soft, golden light. This is your sacred space, a place of infinite creativity and inspiration.

In the center of this clearing stands a beautiful, ancient tree. Its branches stretch up to the sky, connecting the heavens and the earth. You feel drawn to this tree, sensing its deep wisdom and creative power.

**Meeting Your Creative Muse**

As you approach the tree, you notice a figure standing beneath its branches—a being of light and energy, radiating inspiration and creativity. This is your creative muse, the guardian of your creative journey. Take a moment to observe your muse. What do they look like? How do you feel in their presence?

Your muse beckons you closer and invites you to sit with them under the tree. As you sit together, your muse offers you a gift—a key to unlock your creative potential. Accept this gift with gratitude. Hold it in your hands, and feel its energy merging with your own, igniting your creative spirit.

**Dialogue with Your Muse**

Now is the time to communicate with your muse. You may ask them any questions you have about your creative endeavors, seek advice, or simply share your thoughts and feelings. Listen with an open heart to the wisdom they impart. Your muse speaks in a language beyond words, communicating through feelings, images, and sensations. Trust what comes to you.

**Visualizing Your Creative Journey**

With the guidance of your muse, visualize yourself embarking on your creative journey. See yourself working with joy and ease, expressing your creativity freely. Imagine the projects you will create, the challenges you will overcome, and the satisfaction of bringing your visions to life. Feel the support of your muse at every step, guiding and inspiring you.

**Returning to the Present**

It is time to leave this sacred space but know that you can return here anytime you seek inspiration or guidance. Take a deep breath, and as you exhale, begin to bring your awareness back to the present moment. Wiggle your fingers and toes, gently stretch your body, and when you are ready, open your eyes.

Carry the energy and inspiration you have received from your muse into your daily life. Remember, your creative muse is always with you, ready to guide and support you on your creative journey.

*Chapter 7*

# NURTURING INTUITION FOR PERSONAL AND PROFESSIONAL GROWTH

### Embarking on a Meditation Journey to Enhance Intuition

Life is really noisy these days. Cell phones and social media compete for our attention constantly and that is not even taking into account to continual sound pollution that fills the air of this modern world. It is easy for our own voice to get drowned out in the day to day but this inner guide is a priceless asset, steering us towards wise choices, aligning us with our genuine path, and propelling us toward our aspirations. This chapter delves into the profound practice of meditation as a means to not only amplify our intuition but also to awaken our innermost wisdom. It teaches us to be able to lower the volume on external stimuli at will to better hear the directions from your higher self.

Meditation, an ancient practice with deep historical roots, emerges as a guiding light for those yearning to quiet their minds, enhance mindfulness, and establish a deep connection with their true selves. By adopting a consistent meditation routine, we lay the groundwork for our intuition to flourish, offering us a haven from the external noise and chaos, and creating a sacred space where our intuitive voice can resonate clearly.

To begin this meditation journey aimed at boosting your intuition, find a peaceful spot where you can remain undisturbed, making this your sanctuary for daily introspection. Adopt a comfortable position, close your eyes, and take several deep breaths to transition into a state of relaxation, letting go of any stress or tension.

As you become attuned to your breathing, allow each inhalation and exhalation to anchor you in the present moment. Greet your thoughts as they come and go, observing them without attachment, and gently guide your focus back to your breath whenever it wanders.

Turn your attention to your heart, envisioning a glowing light emanating from within, radiating warmth and compassion throughout your being. With each breath, imagine this light growing brighter, enveloping you in its gentle embrace.

In this serene state, introduce a question or intention that resonates with your heart, whether it pertains to your personal journey or professional ambitions. Listen for the wisdom your inner voice imparts, remaining open to the insights that naturally surface, without expectation or judgment.

Commit to this meditation practice regularly, even if for just a few moments each day, and you will soon notice enhanced clarity, a deeper connection with your intuition, and improved decision-making abilities.

Meditation is a deeply personal exploration, unique to every individual who embarks on its path. Approach it with patience and kindness towards yourself, allowing your intuition to unfold naturally. Engaging in meditation offers a powerful ally in both your personal and professional spheres, enabling you to craft a life filled with purpose, joy, and limitless potential.

So, I encourage you now to take a moment, prioritize your well-being, and immerse yourself in the transformative power of meditation. Let the wisdom that lies within guide you towards a life overflowing with purpose, happiness, and infinite possibilities. You do not have to do this perfectly. Simply

## *Journaling and Reflective Practices for Intuitive Growth*

It never ceases to amaze me how many of us our afraid to write. Often we are critiqued by teachers in a way that harms our ability to feely express ourselves without fear of ridicule but for those of us who are spirited women, seekers, entrepreneurs, and pioneers charting our course in the professional world, it is essential to engage in practices that anchor us to our intuition and empower us to flourish in every area of life and work. Among these sacred rituals, journaling and reflective practices stand as powerful tools for transformation. If you are fearful of writing please keep in mind that it really is the same as talking and most of us are comfortable doing that just fine.

Journaling can serve as a refuge, a private space where our deepest thoughts, emotions, and aspirations can be freely expressed on paper. This act of writing acts as a reflective mirror, revealing our deepest desires, fears, and dreams, allowing us to navigate the complexities of our inner landscape. It provides a means to recognize patterns, confront obstacles, and uncover insights about our journey and essence. Beyond its reflective capacity, journaling offers a release, a way to shed the burdens of our emotions and find solace in our own stories.

Reflective practices are the quiet moments we carve out to look inward and contemplate our life's journey, choices, and the steps we have taken along the way. Whether through meditation, mindfulness, or simply granting ourselves the luxury of stillness, these practices deepen our connection to our core. They shine a light on our motivations, highlight opportunities for growth, acknowledge our achievements, and glean wisdom from our challenges. Through reflection, the voice of our intuition becomes clearer, guiding us towards decisions that truly resonate with our essence.

The synergy of combining journaling with reflective practices amplifies the benefits of both. Regularly pouring our hearts onto paper and then reflecting on those words can lead to profound discoveries, creating a cycle of self-awareness and continual personal evolution. This powerful combination nurtures our self-understanding, strengthens our sense of self, and equips us to navigate life's storms with grace and resilience. It opens avenues for setting intentions, tracking our growth, and celebrating our victories, fueling our motivation and charting a path forward.

In "Awaken Your Intuition: Empowering Women for Success in Life and Business," you will find practical tips and guided exercises to harness the power of journaling and reflection. Whether you are already a journaling aficionado or just beginning this journey, this chapter is packed with insights to aid in your exploration of self and bolster your spirit. By integrating these practices into your daily routine, you unlock a gateway to your intuition, revealing the vast potential within and sculpting a life and career in harmony with your truest self.

## *Connecting with Nature to Enhance Intuitive Clarity*

Amidst the digital whirlwind of our contemporary lives, it is surprisingly easy to feel detached from the nurturing embrace of the natural world. Caught in the relentless cycle of daily tasks, carving out moments to pause, reflect, and connect with our inner guidance becomes a cherished rarity. Yet, the soothing call of nature offers a haven, a powerful catalyst for awakening and refining our intuitive senses.

Nature, with her timeless grace, grounds us, drawing us back to the present, to the very essence of our being. When we allow ourselves the simple pleasure of immersing ourselves in the natural world's beauty, we are not merely escaping the noise of our thoughts; we are also tuning into the profound wisdom that lies within.

Mindful walks or hikes in nature provide a wonderful opportunity to commune with the environment for intuitive insights. Each step taken on a forest trail or by the water's edge, fully embracing the sights, sounds, and textures around us, lays the groundwork for our intuition to awaken and speak.

Seeking a tranquil spot within nature's bounty to sit and meditate offers another enriching practice. With eyes closed and deep breaths, feel the earth's supportive presence. As you merge with the elements, allow your intuition to flow freely, guiding your thoughts and revelations. Often, it is in these moments of stillness that clarity and answers effortlessly rise to the surface.

Engaging in outdoor activities like gardening, camping, or simply enjoying the quietude of a park can also act as bridges to our intuitive knowledge. The meditative act of caring for a garden or the peaceful solitude of camping aligns our inner and outer worlds, facilitating access to our intuitive depths.

For those bound to indoor environments, bringing elements of nature indoors through plants, flowers, or natural artifacts can create a serene space conducive to intuitive reflection.

Regularly intertwining our lives with the threads of nature not only ignites our intuitive spark but also deepens our appreciation for the interconnected web of life. As women, seekers, visionaries, and pioneers in our respective fields, leaning into our intuition empowers us to make decisions with confidence, discover creative solutions, and navigate our paths with conviction.

I gently encourage you to step outside, take a deep breath of the world's freshness, and let nature's wisdom guide your intuitive journey. Let the beauty and insights that envelop you fuel your pursuit of success in both your personal life and professional endeavors. Awaken to your intuition and unlock the endless possibilities awaiting discovery.

# Chapter 7 Quests

### *Crafting A Daily Meditation Practice*

Crafting a daily meditation practice is a beautiful journey of self-discovery and intuitive enhancement. Here is a structured approach to building this transformative practice.

Create a Serene Environment: Select a calming space for your daily meditation. Adorn this area with items that evoke tranquility, such as candles, a comfortable cushion, or soothing artwork. This space should serve as your personal sanctuary, a haven from the external world where you can deeply connect with your innermost self.

Commit to Presence and Openness: Begin each meditation session by sitting in a comfortable position that allows for relaxation while keeping your spine straight. Commit to being fully present and open to the experience.

Initiate with Deep Breaths: Start your practice with several deep breaths. Focus on the sensation of air filling your lungs and the subtle pause between inhalation and exhalation. Use this conscious breathing as a gateway to relaxation, signaling your mind and body to release tension.

Visualize Your Intuitive Power: As you breathe, visualize a luminous orb of light in your heart center, representing your intuitive power.

With each breath, imagine this light expanding, illuminating your inner being with wisdom and strength.

Introduce a Question or Intention: Delve deeper into relaxation and introduce a question or intention that holds significance for your journey. This could relate to personal aspirations, professional goals, or spiritual exploration. Allow your consciousness to open to the subtle whispers of your intuition without judgment.

Trust the Process: Understand that this practice is not about seeking immediate answers but about creating a space for insights to emerge organically. Be open to receiving intuitive responses in various forms, such as sensations, emotions, images, or spontaneous thoughts.

Gradually Increase Duration: Start with a manageable duration, such as five minutes, and gradually increase the time as you become more comfortable. Extending your meditation sessions allows you to explore the depths of your intuition more fully.

Journal Post-Meditation: After each session, journal about your experience, noting any insights, feelings, or visions that emerged. This practice helps to solidify your connection with your intuition and serves as a valuable reference for understanding the guidance received over time.

Commit Daily: Dedicate time each day to this practice, recognizing it as a journey of personal evolution. By consistently engaging in meditation, you invite a transformational shift in how you perceive and interact with the world, guided by the rich, intuitive knowledge of your true self.

Embrace this daily meditation practice as a tool for enhancing your intuition and unlocking the profound wisdom within, leading to a life illuminated by insight and serenity.

## *Prompts For Intuitive Journal Writing*

Journaling is a potent tool for enhancing intuition, offering a reflective space to explore your innermost thoughts, feelings, and insights. Here are some inspiring journal writing prompts designed to deepen your intuitive connection and foster a greater understanding of your inner wisdom.

Reflect on a Recent Dream: Describe a recent dream in detail. Explore any symbols, emotions, or messages that appeared. Consider how this dream might be offering guidance or insights into your waking life.

Intuitive Hits of the Day: Write about any intuitive hits or gut feelings you experienced today. Reflect on the circumstances, your reaction, and the outcome. How did following (or not following) these intuitive nudges affect you?

Dialogue with Your Intuition: Write a letter to your intuition as if it were a separate entity. Ask questions about a current dilemma or decision you are facing. Then, write the response from the perspective of your intuition.

Visualize Your Future Self: Imagine yourself in the future, having achieved your dreams and goals. What advice does your future self have for you? Write down any insights or guidance you receive.

Gratitude for Intuitive Guidance: List moments when you felt guided or supported by your intuition in difficult times. Express gratitude for each instance and reflect on how intuition has played a role in your resilience and decision-making.

Explore a Symbol or Sign: Reflect on a symbol, sign, or recurring theme that keeps appearing in your life. Write about its possible meanings and how it might be guiding you on your current path.

Uncover Hidden Feelings: Think about a situation that is causing you confusion or distress. Write freely about your feelings, allowing your intuition to uncover hidden truths or solutions that you had not considered.

Intuitive Creative Expression: Choose a creative medium (writing a poem, sketching, etc.) and let your intuition guide the process. Reflect on the experience and any messages or insights that emerged during this intuitive creative expression.

Revisit a Crossroads Moment: Think back to a time when you stood at a crossroads and had to make a significant decision. With hindsight, reflect on how your intuition influenced your choice. What can you learn from this about trusting your inner guidance?

Set Intentions with Intuitive Guidance: Set an intention for the upcoming week or month. Ask your intuition for guidance on how to best achieve this intention. Write down any steps, feelings, or thoughts that come to you during this reflective process.

Using these prompts, you can cultivate a deeper connection with your intuition, allowing its wisdom to illuminate your path and guide your choices with clarity and confidence.

## *Creative Visualization To Reconnect With Mother Nature*

Reconnecting with mother nature is a profound way to rejuvenate your spirit, ground your energy, and enhance your intuitive connection. This creative visualization exercise is designed to bridge the gap between your inner world and the natural world, helping you to feel more aligned, peaceful, and grounded. Because of the lack of safety for women in the great outdoors I have created this creative visualization to connect with the great power of Gaia indoors.

**Preparation:**

Find a quiet, comfortable place where you will not be disturbed.

Sit or lie down in a relaxed position.

Close your eyes and take a few deep breaths, allowing your body to relax with each exhale.

**Creative Visualization Exercise:**

Begin in a Forest Clearing: Imagine yourself standing in a clearing within a lush, vibrant forest. The sun filters through the canopy, casting dappled shadows on the forest floor. Take a moment to ground yourself here, feeling the earth beneath your feet.

Sense the Elements: Notice the gentle breeze against your skin, carrying the fresh, earthy scent of the forest. Hear the subtle sounds around you—the rustle of leaves, the distant call of birds, the soft murmur of a nearby stream.

Walk Towards the Stream: Begin to walk slowly towards the sound of the water. With each step, feel yourself becoming more connected to the natural world around you. Notice the vibrant colors of the plants and trees, the texture of the earth beneath your feet, and the cool, moist air as you approach the stream.

Reach the Stream: Upon arriving at the stream, take a moment to observe the water's flow. Notice how it moves effortlessly over rocks and around obstacles, always finding the easiest path forward. Reflect on how this mirrors your own life's journey, flowing around challenges and moving towards your goals.

Interact with the Water: Imagine kneeling beside the stream and gently placing your hands in the water. Feel its coolness, its vitality, energizing your being. As you touch the water, imagine it washing away any worries, tension, or negative energy, leaving you refreshed and renewed.

Connect with the Earth: Now, place your hands on the earth beside the stream. Feel its stability, its nurturing energy. Imagine drawing strength and nourishment from the earth, grounding yourself deeply in the present moment.

Absorb the Forest's Wisdom: Look around the forest once more, recognizing it as a living, breathing entity filled with ancient wisdom. Open your heart and mind to receive any messages or insights the forest may have for you. This could come as a feeling, a word, an image, or simply a sense of knowing.

Thank the Natural World: Take a moment to express your gratitude to the forest, the stream, and all the life forms around you for their beauty, inspiration, and wisdom.

Return to the Present: Begin to walk back to the forest clearing, carrying with you the peace and connection you have found. Gradually bring your awareness back to your physical surroundings, wiggling your fingers and toes, and when you are ready, open your eyes.

## Integration

After completing the visualization, take a few moments to journal about your experience. Note any feelings, insights, or inspirations that arose.

If possible, spend some time in nature soon, allowing your physical senses to deepen the connection you have cultivated through this visualization.

This exercise serves as a bridge, allowing you to draw the serene, grounding energy of nature into your daily life, enhancing your overall well-being and intuitive clarity.

# Chapter 8

# INTUITION AND SELF-CARE

### Embracing Our Inner Guide

As women, navigating the multifaceted roles we play, from professionals to solopreneurs, the quest for external achievements can sometimes overshadow the powerful ally within us—our intuition. We get so caught up in the world of material success that we forget to honor the very mechanism that helps us achieve that, our relationship with our inner world.

"Awaken Your Intuition: Empowering Women for Success in Life and Business" invites us on a journey to rediscover and harness this inner wisdom as a guiding light towards success. This section, "Embracing Our Inner Guide," serves as a reminder of the transformative power of tuning into our intuitive voices.

Acknowledging our intuition begins with recognizing its existence and its capacity to guide us beyond the realms of logic and reason.

It is that gentle nudge, the voice that whispers truths in moments of silence, offering clarity and direction. By valuing and trusting this inner wisdom, we cultivate a deeper sense of self-trust, enhance our decision-making, and live more authentically.

We delve into various practices that facilitate a closer bond with our intuition, highlighting mindfulness, meditation, and reflection as gateways to quieting the mind and allowing our intuitive knowledge to surface. This exploration underscores the importance of intuition in guiding our choices, celebrating the instinctual pulls that lead us towards fulfilling paths.

Moreover, this section explores the crucial role of self-care and love in nurturing our intuitive selves. It emphasizes the need for dedicating time to activities that nourish our souls, advocating for self-compassion and the pursuit of joy as foundations for a flourishing intuitive connection.

Real-life stories and practical exercises are introduced later, offering women tools to strengthen their relationship with their intuition. Through journaling prompts, guided meditations, and intuitive exercises, readers are encouraged to dive deep into their inner sanctums, embracing the wisdom found within.

"Embracing Our Inner Guide" is a call to women to embark on a journey of self-discovery and empowerment, highlighting that within each of us lies a wellspring of wisdom waiting to be explored. By inviting our intuition into our daily lives, we navigate life's complexities with greater clarity, confidence, and success. Let's walk this path together, awakening our intuition to sculpt a life and career that resonate deeply with our truest desires.

## *The Healing Power of Self-Intuition*

In the pursuit of personal and professional fulfillment, the art of tapping into our inner wisdom and embracing self-healing emerges as foundational. Amid the hustle of achieving and becoming, the subtle voice of our intuition and the transformative potential of self-healing often go unnoticed. This chapter shines a light on the paths to accessing these inner strengths, guiding us to victories in both our personal endeavors and professional journeys.

Our intuition acts as a direct line to the subconscious, offering insights that bypass conventional logic, enabling us to make decisions with a blend of clarity and confidence. This section introduces a variety of practices, including journaling, meditation, and mindfulness, aimed at fostering a deeper connection with ourselves and uncovering the rich wisdom residing within.

The essence of self-healing is also pivotal, urging us to prioritize our well-being amidst life's demands. It calls us to address our physical, emotional, and spiritual health with the utmost care, employing techniques such as energy healing, breathwork, and visualization to release emotional burdens, heal from past traumas, and enhance our vitality.

By weaving self-intuition and self-healing into our daily routines, we empower ourselves to overcome challenges, make resonant decisions, and cultivate inner peace. This journey not only influences our personal growth but also enriches our professional lives, relationships, and the overall blueprint of our success.

For those charting new territories in entrepreneurship or on a voyage of self-discovery, this chapter serves as a guide, offering practical advice, exercises, and wisdom to ignite the flame of intuition and foster self-healing. It equips you with the knowledge and tools to awaken your intuitive potential and harness your inner healing power, paving the way for growth, purpose, and fulfillment.

Step into this exploration of self-reflection and healing, unlocking the vast potential within. Empower yourself to navigate life's choices with insight, heal from within, and manifest a life and career that truly reflects your deepest aspirations.

## *Harmonizing Intuition with Rational Thought*

In the intricate dance of self-evolution and discovery, mastering the balance between intuition and logic emerges as a key to wholeness. These two forces, often seen in opposition, are in fact complementary, each enhancing the other to guide women through life's and business's complexities with grace. This chapter explores the harmony between intuition and logic, shining a light on how embracing both can empower us to awaken our intuitive selves fully.

Intuition, our internal compass, offers a direct connection to our deepest knowings, guiding us through feelings, hunches, and heart whispers. It invites us to trust in paths that may not be immediately logical but feel profoundly right, enriching our lives with creativity, insight, and authenticity.

Logic, on the other hand, provides the structure to our thoughts, helping us to analyze, plan, and execute decisions with clarity and precision. It grounds our flights of intuition, ensuring our dreams and visions can be realized in practical, tangible ways.

Merging intuition with logic and reason creates a powerful toolkit for navigating life's decisions. This synergy allows us to uncover passions, seize aligned opportunities, and face challenges with a blend of courage and pragmatism. For those on spiritual or self-discovery journeys, this balance deepens our connection to our intuition while keeping us anchored in practical reality.

For entrepreneurs and professionals, this blend is invaluable. Intuition can reveal new trends, deepen audience connections, and inspire innovative decisions, while logic ensures strategies are grounded, adaptable, and sustainable.

By fostering a partnership between intuition and logic, women across all spheres can tap into their fullest potential, making enlightened choices that reflect both their inner voice and the demands of the external world. This chapter invites us to embrace this journey, discovering the transformative power of uniting our intuition with rational thought for a life and career of true fulfillment and success. Let us explore this path, awakening our intuition and grounding it in wisdom, to realize the profound impact it can have on our lives.

# Chapter 8 Quests

## *The Marriage Of Heart And Mind Exercise*

The cooperation between intuition and intellect creates a powerful synergy for decision-making, problem-solving, and personal growth. This meditation exercise is designed to harmonize these aspects of your mind, fostering a balanced approach to life's challenges and opportunities.

### Preparation

Find a quiet, comfortable place where you can sit or lie down without interruptions.

Set aside 15-20 minutes for this exercise.

Begin with a few deep, cleansing breaths to center yourself.

### Meditation Exercise:

### Relaxation and Centering

Close your eyes and focus on your breath. Inhale deeply and exhale slowly, allowing your body to relax with each breath.

With every exhale, release any tension you are holding in your body. Feel yourself becoming more relaxed and centered.

## Visualizing the Mind's Aspects

Imagine a space within you where your intuition and logic can meet. Visualize this as a serene garden, a tranquil meeting room, or any setting that feels harmonious and balanced.

In one part of this space, visualize your intuitive self. This may appear as a light, a feeling, or a symbolic image representing intuition's fluidity and depth.

In another part of the space, visualize your logical self. This might take the form of structured light, geometric shapes, or any representation that embodies logic's clarity and order.

## Dialogue Between Intuition and Logic

Imagine these aspects of your mind beginning to communicate with each other. They do so with respect, curiosity, and openness, each valuing the other's perspective.

Notice how your intuitive self communicates—not just in words but in feelings, images, and sensations.

Observe how your logical self contributes, offering structured thoughts, analyses, and clarity.

## Finding Synergy

Now, bring a current question or challenge into this space. Present it to both your intuitive and logical selves.

Allow each aspect to offer its perspective. First, listen to your intuition—what feelings or gut reactions arise? What deeper understandings emerge?

Then, turn to your logic. What analysis, facts, or rational thoughts come forward?

Imagine these insights blending together, forming a more comprehensive understanding or solution that honors both your intuition and your logic.

## Integration

Visualize this integrated insight forming a radiant orb of light or energy in the center of your internal space, symbolizing the harmony between your intuition and logic.

Imagine this light expanding, filling your entire being, illuminating your mind with balanced wisdom.

## Closing the Meditation

Take a few deep breaths, bringing the sense of harmony and balance back with you into your everyday consciousness.

When you are ready, gently open your eyes, feeling refreshed, balanced, and ready to approach your decisions and challenges with a harmonized perspective.

## After the Exercise

Reflect on the experience in your journal. Note any insights, feelings, or resolutions that emerged during the meditation.

Consider how you might apply this balanced approach to specific areas of your life, enhancing your decision-making process with a blend of intuition and logic.

This meditation serves as a bridge, uniting the profound depths of your intuition with the clear light of your logic, empowering you to navigate life with a holistic and balanced perspective.

## Tips To Recharge For Empaths And Intuitives

Empaths, with their heightened sensitivity to the emotions and energies of those around them, often need specialized self-healing practices to maintain their well-being and protect their energy. Here is a list of ten self-healing ideas tailored for empaths to help restore balance, rejuvenate their energy, and strengthen their emotional boundaries:

Grounding Techniques: Practice grounding exercises such as walking barefoot on the earth, meditating with grounding crystals (like black tourmaline or hematite), or visualizing roots extending from your feet deep into the ground. Grounding helps to release excess energy and reconnect with the stabilizing energy of the earth.

Energy Shielding Visualization: Visualize a protective shield of light around your body, intending that this shield allows positive energy in while deflecting and neutralizing any negativity. This can be particularly useful before entering crowded or energetically charged environments.

Scheduled Alone Time: Regularly schedule periods of solitude to disconnect from the energies of others and recharge your own. Use this time for activities that nourish your soul, such as reading, journaling, or practicing a hobby.

Nature Reconnection: Spend time in nature to cleanse your energy and rejuvenate your spirit. The natural world offers a unique, calming energy that can help empaths find balance and peace.

Cleansing Baths: Take salt baths with Epsom or Pink Himalayan salt to cleanse your aura and draw out any negativity absorbed from others. Incorporating lavender or sage essential oils can enhance the cleansing and relaxation effects.

Breathwork and Meditation: Regular breathwork exercises and meditation can help center your thoughts and emotions, allowing you to detach from external energies and focus on inner peace.

Expressive Arts: Engage in expressive arts therapy, such as painting, writing, or dancing, to process and release emotions in a constructive and creative way. Artistic expression can be a powerful tool for emotional healing and self-discovery.

Energy Healing Practices: Explore energy healing techniques such as Reiki, acupuncture, or Qi Gong to manage and balance your energy fields. These practices can help clear blockages and enhance your emotional and physical well-being.

Healthy Emotional Boundaries: Practice setting and maintaining healthy emotional boundaries with others. Learn to say no when needed and prioritize your own well-being without feeling guilty for taking care of yourself.

Seek Supportive Communities: Connect with groups or communities that understand and support empathic sensitivities. Sharing experiences and coping strategies with like-minded individuals can offer comfort and practical advice for managing your energy.

Implementing these self-healing practices can help empaths navigate their sensitivities more effectively, ensuring that they can continue to embrace their empathic gifts without feeling overwhelmed or drained.

*Chapter 9*

# INTUITION FOR PERSONAL GROWTH AND TRANSFORMATION

### *Tuning In for Self-Discovery*

I n the ever-accelerating dance of life, where days blend into nights and moments of quiet reflection are as rare as rain in the desert, the act of listening to our intuition becomes not just beneficial, but essential. This innate guide, particularly resonant within women, serves as our compass through life's complexities, aligning our actions with the deepest truths of our soul. This segment, "Tuning In for Self-Discovery," is dedicated to the exploration of intuition as a key to unlocking our full potential, empowering women to thrive in every aspect of their existence, from personal well-being to professional achievements.

Intuition speaks the language of feelings, an emotional intelligence that women naturally excel in. However, the constant buzz of life often mutes these internal whispers. Learning to tune into and value our intuitive insights allows us to explore the hidden depths of our being, uncovering passions, strengths, and aspirations previously obscured.

The journey of self-discovery through intuition encourages us to find moments of silence amidst the noise, to meditate, reflect, and practice mindfulness. In these spaces of calm, our authentic desires and truths emerge with clarity, guiding our steps with a sense of purpose and authenticity.

For entrepreneurs and professionals, intuition becomes an invaluable tool, informing decisions, nurturing connections, and sparking innovation. It provides a unique lens through which to view opportunities and challenges, enriching our professional paths with wisdom beyond the grasp of logic.

Moreover, in moments of doubt and uncertainty, our intuition shines as a beacon, offering direction and a deep sense of knowing. It encourages us to trust our instincts, to step forward with confidence, aligning our professional journey with our personal values and dreams.

This section introduces practical advice to empower women to connect with their intuition for self-discovery. Through journaling, visualization, and intuitive exercises, we are invited to delve into our inner world, embracing the insights and wisdom that surface.

By awakening our intuition, we enable ourselves to craft lives and careers filled with purpose, joy, and achievement. Whether you are a seeker, an entrepreneur, or a professional navigating your path, engaging with your intuition can transform your approach to life and business. Let us embark on this journey of self-discovery, unlocking the vast potential within to shape the life and career we truly desire.

## Manifesting Desires with Intuitive Insight

Amid the rush of our roles as visionaries, entrepreneurs, and professionals, carving out time for introspection and personal growth often falls by the wayside. Yet, at the heart of our hustle lies a dormant power waiting to be unleashed—our intuition. This deep, silent wisdom whispers not only the path to success but also a journey filled with fulfillment and joy across every area of our lives.

Intuition is our direct line to the subconscious, a beacon guiding us toward decisions that deeply resonate on a personal and professional level. Yet, in the whirlwind of societal expectations and daily responsibilities, this intuitive essence is often neglected.

"Manifesting Your Desires with Intuitive Insight" encourages women to reclaim their intuitive strength. It is about shaping our deepest aspirations into tangible realities, creating a life imbued with abundance and happiness.

This chapter invites you to engage in transformative practices that strengthen your intuitive connection, teaching you to quit external distractions to hear your inner voice. Through visualization, meditation, and reflective journaling, you are guided to uncover your true desires and chart a course towards their realization.

Furthermore, we delve into the power of intention-setting, aligning thoughts and actions with your heart's desires. We explore the energy realm, learning to elevate our vibrational state to attract positive experiences and opportunities our way.

Featuring inspiring stories of women who have turned their dreams into reality by tapping into their intuition, this chapter stands as proof of the limitless potential within. These stories are not just narratives; they are beacons of possibility, affirming that you, too, can shape your desires into the fabric of your life.

By embracing the wisdom of intuition, you step into a realm where decisions are made with confidence, your life reflects abundance, and your journey is marked by fulfillment. Whether you are embarking on a personal evolution, building your business, or seeking enlightenment, this chapter is your guide to a life where dreams and reality merge, all led by the silent yet powerful voice within.

## *Navigating Change with Intuitive Grace*

Change, the only constant, sculpts the narrative of our lives, threading through our personal and professional worlds. As women navigating diverse roles—from seekers to entrepreneurs, professionals to visionaries—the waves of change are familiar companions. Yet, it is in our dance with change, our transformation, that our true strength to thrive in life and business is revealed.

In "Navigating Change with Intuitive Grace," we delve into embracing change not as a harbinger of disruption but as an ally for growth, discovery, and empowerment. This journey unveils the transformative power change wields, guiding us through life's and career's shifting landscapes with poise and confidence.

Change often arrives draped in uncertainty, sparking resistance born from fear of the unknown. Yet, envisioning change as an opportunity for growth invites a paradigm shift, opening us to experiences and paths rich with potential for personal and professional fulfillment.

This section offers strategies and insights for gracefully navigating change, highlighting the role of self-reflection, mindfulness, and intuition in steering through transitions with intention and authenticity. By aligning our choices with our inner wisdom, we embark on a journey marked by clarity, resilience, and alignment with our true selves.

Furthermore, we explore the significance of a growth mindset in transforming challenges into opportunities for evolution. Practical exercises and tools are shared to strengthen this mindset, empowering us to face change with resilience and grace.

The journey through change is enriched by the community—connecting with like-minded individuals provides strength and inspiration. This chapter guides on fostering these valuable connections, creating a support network that uplifts and sustains us through the winds of change.

To dance with change is to unlock our fullest potential, weaving a story of triumph in both personal and professional realms. With self-reflection, mindfulness, intuition, a resilient mindset, and the warmth of community, we can navigate the seas of change with elegance and strength. "Navigating Change with Intuitive Grace" invites you to awaken your intuition and harness the transformative power of change, charting a course towards success and fulfillment. Let us embrace this journey together, discovering the limitless horizons of our potential.

# Chapter 9 Quests

## *A Spiritual Contract Between a Woman and Her Intuition*

This contract is a sacred agreement, forged in the ethereal realms of understanding and connection, between the essence of my being and the divine gift of my intuition. It serves as a testament to the powerful bond I wish to nurture and honor throughout my journey in this lifetime. By affirming this contract, I commit to the following principles and practices, thereby strengthening the bridge between my conscious self and the profound wisdom that lies within.

Article I: Acknowledgment of Intuition as a Guiding Force

I, [Woman's Name], recognize my intuition as an inherent, guiding force, a whisper from the universe, and my soul's language. I acknowledge it as my most trusted advisor, a source of insight and foresight that transcends the limitations of logical reasoning.

Article II: Commitment to Trust

I vow to trust the gentle nudges, the subtle signs, and the powerful gut feelings that guide me towards my highest good. I pledge to honor these internal signals, even when they defy conventional wisdom, knowing they are the compass of my soul.

## Article III: Practice of Mindfulness and Stillness

I commit to cultivating moments of stillness and mindfulness in my daily life, creating a fertile ground for my intuition to flourish. Through meditation, contemplation, and reflection, I shall open the channels of communication with my inner wisdom.

## Article IV: Courage to Act on Intuition

I promise to embrace the courage required to act upon my intuitive insights, understanding that each step taken in alignment with my inner guidance is a step towards my true destiny. I recognize that this courage strengthens my trust in myself and the universe.

## Article V: Dedication to Self-Care and Boundaries

I acknowledge the importance of self-care and the establishment of healthy boundaries in nurturing my intuitive abilities. By taking care of my physical, emotional, and spiritual well-being, I enhance my sensitivity and receptivity to intuitive messages.

## Article VI: Continuous Learning and Openness

I pledge to remain open to the lessons and messages my intuition provides, viewing challenges as opportunities for growth and deeper understanding. I commit to being a lifelong learner of the language of my soul.

Article VII: Gratitude and Recognition

I express profound gratitude for the gift of intuition and for every instance it has guided, protected, and enlightened me. I promise to acknowledge and celebrate the ways in which my intuition enriches my life.

Article VIII: Sharing of Wisdom

Understanding the power of shared experiences, I vow to share the wisdom gained from my intuitive journey with others, when guided to do so, fostering a collective elevation of consciousness.

Closing Affirmation:

I hereby seal this spiritual contract with my intuition, affirming its validity and significance from this moment forward. May the bond between us grow ever stronger, illuminating my path with clarity, love, and wisdom. May I walk through life empowered by the knowledge that I am never alone, for my intuition is an eternal guide and companion.

Signed with love and commitment,

[Signature]

[Date]

This spiritual contract is a living document, open to evolution and recommitment, as I grow and journey forward on my path of self-discovery and spiritual enlightenment.

## *Guided Visualization to Develop Trust in Your Intuition*

### Grounding and Centering

Close your eyes and take three deep, slow breaths. Inhale peace and calm, exhale any tension or stress.

Imagine roots growing from the soles of your feet, extending deep into the earth. Feel grounded, stable, and supported.

Visualize a beam of luminous energy descending from the sky, entering the top of your head, filling your body with light and clarity. This light anchors you in the present moment, preparing you for intuitive connection.

### Meeting Your Intuitive Self

Envision yourself walking on a path in a serene forest. The trees sway gently in the breeze, birds sing harmoniously, and sunlight filters through the leaves, creating patterns on the ground.

As you walk, notice a clearing ahead with a comfortable seat in the center. Approach this seat and take a moment to sit down.

Sitting here, call forth your intuitive self. This may appear as a figure, a light, or simply a sensation. Greet this aspect of yourself with openness and curiosity.

### Dialogue with Your Intuition

Ask your intuitive self what it needs from you to strengthen your trust in it. Listen attentively to the response, which may come as words, feelings, or images.

Inquire about any fears or doubts you have about trusting your intuition. Allow your intuitive self to offer guidance, reassurance, or healing insights.

Discuss with your intuitive self how you can better recognize and honor its guidance in your daily life.

### Receiving a Symbol of Trust

Request from your intuitive self a symbol representing trust and confidence in your intuition. This could be an object, a color, or a symbol.

Imagine yourself receiving this symbol with gratitude. Place it in your heart, knowing it will serve as a reminder of your connection and trust in your intuition.

### Integrating and Returning

Spend a few moments breathing deeply, allowing the insights and energies from this encounter to integrate into your being.

Gradually, begin to bring your awareness back to the present moment. Wiggle your fingers and toes, stretch gently, and when you feel ready, open your eyes.

Carry the symbol of trust with you in your heart, ready to consult it whenever you seek guidance or reassurance from your intuition.

### Reflection and Journaling

After completing this visualization, you may wish to journal about your experience. Write down the symbol you received, the insights from your dialogue, and any feelings that arose. Reflecting on these can further solidify your connection to your intuition and help you recognize its presence more readily in your life.

Remember, developing trust in your intuition is a journey. Regularly engaging with practices like this visualization can deepen your intuitive abilities and enhance your overall sense of inner guidance and wisdom.

Drawing upon the powerful technique of creative visualization combined with the practice of intuitive journaling, here is a bespoke exercise designed to harness your intuition for manifesting your goals:

## *Intuitive Visualization Journaling for Goal Manifestation*

### Objective

To use your intuition and visualization skills to manifest a specific goal or desire in your life.

### Materials Needed

A journal or notebook

A quiet, comfortable space where you won't be disturbed

Step 1: Grounding and Centering

Begin by finding a quiet space where you can sit comfortably without interruptions.

Close your eyes, take deep breaths, and visualize roots extending from your feet into the earth, grounding you. Feel a sense of calm and presence.

## Step 2: Clearing Your Mind

Continue breathing deeply and with each exhale, release any tension, stress, or preoccupations.

Visualize a clear, open sky or a calm body of water, symbolizing a clear mind ready for intuitive insights.

## Step 3: Setting Your Intention

Open your eyes and, in your journal, write down a goal or desire you wish to manifest. Be as specific as possible.

Underneath, write why this goal is important to you and how achieving it would make you feel. This connects your intention with emotion, a powerful catalyst for manifestation.

## Step 4: Creative Visualization

Close your eyes again, and with the goal in mind, begin to visualize the scenario in which your goal has already been achieved.

Engage all your senses in this visualization. What do you see, hear, smell, touch, and feel? Imagine the emotions of joy, fulfillment, and gratitude washing over you as if your goal has already manifested.

Allow this scene to unfold naturally in your mind, paying attention to any intuitive nudges or additional details your subconscious brings forth.

### Step 5: Intuitive Journaling

Open your eyes and return to your journal. Now, write down any insights, symbols, ideas, or steps that came to you during your visualization. These could be actions you need to take, people to connect with, or new perspectives to adopt.

Trust your intuition to guide your writing. This is your inner wisdom communicating with you.

### Step 6: Actionable Steps

Reflect on your intuitive journaling and identify actionable steps that you can take towards your goal. Write these down in a list format.

Make a commitment to yourself to take at least one small step each day or week towards your goal, guided by the intuition captured in your journal.

### Step 7: Daily Affirmation

Create a positive affirmation related to your goal and write it down. For example, "I am confidently taking steps towards achieving [your goal], and I trust my intuition to guide me."

Repeat this affirmation daily, especially before journaling or visualization sessions, to reinforce your intention and belief in your ability to manifest your goal.

Regular Practice:

Engage in this exercise regularly, ideally at the start or end of your day. Over time, you will strengthen your intuitive connection and manifest your goals with greater ease and clarity.

Remember, the key to this exercise is trust—trust in yourself, your intuition, and the process of manifestation. Through consistent practice, you will not only move closer to achieving your goals but also deepen your intuitive abilities.

*Chapter 10*

# EMPOWERING WOMEN THROUGH INTUITION

## *Celebrating Feminine Wisdom*

In a man's world that often prizes logic and analytical might, the call for women to reconnect with their inherent intuitive power rings with increasing urgency. Intuition, our inner "sixth sense," serves as a guiding light, steering us through life's decisions, unveiling our deepest passions, and charting paths of success in both our personal and professional spheres. This chapter, "Celebrating Feminine Wisdom," is an ode to the journey of embracing and harnessing feminine intuition, a path leading to empowerment and the realization of our fullest potential.

For women, intuition is not just a skill but a natural extension of our being, capable of offering insights and understanding beyond the reach of our conscious minds. Yet, the noise and demands of daily life can often muffle this inner voice. By learning to listen to and honor these intuitive whispers, we unlock a treasure trove of creativity, wisdom, and strength.

Embarking on this journey requires us to cultivate spaces of quiet and mindfulness, allowing us to connect with our intuition more deeply. Whether through meditation, reflective practices, or simply pausing to tune into our feelings, we begin to align our actions with our authentic selves, leading to a life of purpose and satisfaction.

In the realm of business and entrepreneurship, intuition emerges as a powerful ally, shedding light on opportunities, guiding strategic decisions, and nurturing connections. It offers a unique advantage, marrying our professional endeavors with our inner values and passions.

But the significance of intuition extends beyond career milestones; it is a holistic approach that enriches every facet of life. From fostering meaningful relationships to advocating for self-care and personal growth, intuition guides us toward choices that honor our well-being and happiness.

This chapter unveils methods and practices to ignite and strengthen women's intuitive abilities. Through meditation, journaling, and energy healing, among others, we are invited to explore and trust the wisdom that lies within, unlocking our limitless potential.

By embracing our feminine intuition, we step into a flow of inner knowing, utilizing our unique gifts to craft lives of authenticity and alignment. It is a source of empowerment, urging women to rise in all aspects of life, and this narrative is your guide to unlocking the profound gifts of your intuitive essence.

## *Redefining Success Beyond Boundaries*

In a landscape long shaped by patriarchal narratives and laden with gendered expectations, women have navigated through a myriad of constraints, both visible and subtle, in their personal journeys and professional aspirations. Today, we stand at the threshold of change, ready to harness our inner power and transcend these limitations. "Redefining Success Beyond Boundaries" is a testament to this shift, offering insights and strategies to empower women to break free from traditional molds and embrace their full potential.

The first step in this transformative journey involves challenging and reshaping the limiting beliefs and societal expectations that have historically defined women's roles. Recognizing these narratives as constructs rather than truths empowers us to forge our own definitions of success, unbound by gendered stereotypes.

Venturing into traditionally male-dominated fields, women are not just breaking stereotypes but are also paving the way for future generations, proving that our capabilities extend far beyond societal constraints. By claiming our space in all spheres, we dismantle outdated perceptions and inspire a movement of equality and empowerment.

This journey also involves a profound exploration of self, challenging societal measures of worth and embracing our unique identities with love and acceptance. This self-revelation not only fosters personal growth but also fuels our professional endeavors with authenticity and confidence.

Embracing this path requires courage, resilience, and a steadfast belief in our abilities. As we collectively challenge and transcend these barriers, we not only liberate ourselves but also light the way for others, fostering a culture of empowerment and inclusivity.

## Uplifting Through Collective Wisdom

While women's accension has risen across various domains, the significance of fostering a supportive and empowering network cannot be overstated. "Uplifting Through Collective Wisdom" underscores the importance of solidarity among women, recognizing that our journey towards empowerment is interconnected. By sharing knowledge, resources, and encouragement, we create an ecosystem where every woman has the opportunity to flourish.

The essence of this support lies in understanding that our successes and challenges are shared, moving beyond competition to embrace collaboration. Mentorship programs, networking groups, and shared spaces offer platforms for women to connect, learn, and grow together.

Celebrating each other's achievements plays a crucial role in this supportive framework. Highlighting the successes of fellow women not only inspires but also reinforces the belief in our collective potential. By amplifying women's voices and stories, we challenge prevailing narratives and showcase the diverse capabilities and strengths within our community.

Active listening and empathy are foundational to this support system. Our intuitive nature equips us to genuinely connect with and understand the experiences of others, offering solace and guidance. In fostering these empathetic connections, we build a network of mutual support and inspiration.

Empowering one another through intuition, collaboration, and celebration transforms individual achievements into collective progress. As we navigate our personal and professional journeys, let us remember the power of our united efforts and the transformative impact of nurturing sisterhood. Together, we forge a path of empowerment, setting a precedent for future generations and reshaping the landscape of possibility for women everywhere.

# Chapter 10 Quest

### *Famous Women Who Used Their Intuition*

Intuition plays a critical role in guiding decisions in life and business, and many successful women credit their intuitive insights for their accomplishments. Here is a list of famous women known for harnessing the power of their intuition in their careers and personal lives:

Coco Chanel: The founder of the Chanel brand, Coco Chanel revolutionized the fashion industry with her intuitive sense of style and understanding of what women wanted from fashion, moving away from the restrictive corsets of the time to more comfortable and practical attire.

Marie Curie: A pioneer in the field of radioactivity, Marie Curie's intuition led her to discoveries that earned her two Nobel Prizes in Physics and Chemistry. Her intuitive grasp of scientific concepts was far ahead of her time.

Eleanor Roosevelt: As a political figure and activist, Eleanor Roosevelt trusted her intuition in advocating for human rights, women's issues, and the welfare of youth, becoming a powerful influence in American politics.

**Florence Nightingale:** Known as the founder of modern nursing, Florence Nightingale's intuition guided her to implement sanitary hospital practices during the Crimean War, drastically reducing death rates. Her insights transformed nursing into a respected profession.

**Rosalind Franklin:** Her intuition and expertise in X-ray crystallography led to the discovery of the DNA double helix structure, a monumental achievement in understanding genetic material, even though her contribution was only widely recognized posthumously.

**Ada Lovelace:** Often considered the world's first computer programmer, Ada Lovelace's intuition and understanding of mathematics led her to conceptualize the first algorithm intended to be processed by a machine.

**Harriet Tubman:** An abolitionist and political activist, Harriet Tubman relied on her intuition and courage to guide dozens of slaves to freedom through the Underground Railroad, despite immense danger.

**Agatha Christie:** The best-selling novelist of all time, Agatha Christie used her intuition to craft intricate plots and memorable characters, making her the "Queen of Mystery."

**Mother Teresa:** A symbol of compassion and charity, Mother Teresa followed her intuition to serve the poor, sick, and dying in Kolkata, India, leading to the establishment of the Missionaries of Charity.

**Queen Elizabeth I:** As the monarch of England during a time of religious turmoil and external threats, Elizabeth I's intuitive leadership and political acumen steered her country into a period of peace and prosperity known as the Elizabethan Era.

Oprah Winfrey: One of the most influential women in the world, Oprah has often spoken about the importance of listening to her intuition across her multifaceted career as a talk show host, media proprietor, and philanthropist.

Arianna Huffington: Co-founder of The Huffington Post and founder of Thrive Global, Arianna has written about the significance of intuition in making business decisions and the role it played in her success.

Sara Blakely: The founder of Spanx, Sara Blakely, has credited trusting her gut feelings as a crucial element in her journey from selling fax machines to becoming a self-made billionaire and transforming the women's undergarment industry.

Indra Nooyi: The former CEO of PepsiCo, Indra Nooyi, has discussed how intuition influenced her leadership style and decision-making process, helping to navigate the company through numerous innovative changes.

Sheryl Sandberg: As COO of Facebook and author of "Lean In," Sheryl Sandberg has emphasized the importance of gut feelings in career choices and leadership, advocating for women to trust their instincts.

Ginni Rometty: The former CEO of IBM, Ginni Rometty, has spoken about the role of intuition in her leadership, particularly in the fast-evolving tech industry, where intuitive foresight can guide innovation.

Mary Barra: As the CEO of General Motors, Mary Barra has led the company through significant transitions, emphasizing the importance of intuition in her leadership decisions, especially regarding the automotive industry's future.

Beyoncé Knowles-Carter: An iconic figure in music and business, Beyoncé has often credited her intuition for her bold choices in her career and personal brand, demonstrating the power of intuitive insight in the creative industry.

These women, among so many others, exemplify how intuition can be a powerful ally in navigating the complexities of life and business, offering insights that logic alone may not provide. Their achievements underscore the value of listening to one's inner voice and trusting it as a guide.

*Chapter 11*

# INTUITION IN LIFE'S CHALLENGES

## *Guided by Inner Wisdom in Tough Times*

Life is by it's very nature feels uncertain. Challenges loom and the path ahead seems shrouded in mist, our intuition emerges as a guiding light, a silent ally whispering truths into the heart of our struggles. "Guided by Inner Wisdom in Tough Times," a cornerstone of "Awaken Your Intuition: Empowering Women for Success in Life and Business," explores the pivotal role of intuition in navigating life's more challenging chapters. This discourse invites us into a deeper engagement with our intuitive selves, illuminating the path for women across various spheres to find direction and solace amidst adversity.

Our intuition is like a quiet pulse within, often overshadowed by the louder voices of logic and reason. Yet, it is in moments of uncertainty that this subtle guide can cut through the confusion, offering insights and clarity when traditional navigational tools fall short. Learning to lean into our intuitive senses, to trust the gentle nudges and the knowledge that bubbles up from within, arms us with the confidence to traverse even the most daunting of life's passages.

This section delves into practices that awaken and fortify our connection to intuition. From the reflective sanctuaries of meditation to the grounding practices of mindfulness, we uncover avenues that not only nurture our intuitive voice but also provide a haven from life's storms. Emphasizing the importance of self-care, it invites us to indulge in rituals that rejuvenate our spirit, allowing for a clearer channel to our inner wisdom.

Moreover, we explore the transformative act of embracing life's ebb and flow. Recognizing that resistance often amplifies turmoil, surrendering to the journey and trusting in the unfolding of our path allows us to navigate with grace and resilience. This surrender does not signify defeat but an alignment with the rhythms of life, guided by the certainty that our intuition will lead us to our desired shore.

Embarking on the path of intuitive decision-making during tumultuous times not only empowers us to face challenges with dignity but also enriches our journey with insights and growth. By fostering a deep bond with our inner wisdom, embracing self-nurturance, and learning to flow with life's inevitable changes, we unlock the doors to navigating life's challenges with assurance and heart.

## *Embracing Uncertainty with Intuitive Trust*

For most of us navigating the stressful terrain of modern life it seems that certainty is a rare gem and change the only constant. And exactly for those reasons the significance of trusting our intuition cannot be overstated. "Embracing Uncertainty with Intuitive Trust" delves into the heart of relying on our inner compass during times of flux, spotlighting the profound impact this trust can have on women in every arena, from the personal to the professional.

For women, embracing our intuitive power is not merely beneficial; it is essential. It connects us to a reservoir of wisdom, enabling a deep communion with our desires, dreams, and decisions. Our intuition acts as a guiding light, offering direction even when the path ahead is veiled in obscurity. By honoring these inner signals, we unlock the capacity to navigate life's uncertainties with a sense of purpose and poise.

This journey of intuitive trust challenges the primacy of rational thought, inviting us to explore beyond the tangible and the known. Through meditation, journaling, and tuning into our bodily sensations, we cultivate a dialogue with our intuition, learning to discern its guidance amidst life's noise.

Furthermore, this chapter illuminates the importance of fostering a mindset open to intuition. Embracing a belief in our inner knowledge as a dependable guide, we can approach decisions with confidence, transforming the unknown into a landscape of potential and growth.

"Embracing Uncertainty with Intuitive Trust" is a testament to the strength and clarity intuition offers women across all facets of life. Through practical tips and inspiring narratives, this section serves as a beacon for those ready to harness their intuitive strength, guiding them through the unpredictable journey of life with wisdom and grace.

## Finding Direction with Intuitive Insight

For most of us women living in the adult world, decisions loom large and the pressure to choose wisely is ever-present. It is here that intuition stands as a sanctuary of wisdom and insight. "Finding Direction with Intuitive Insight" explores the invaluable role of intuition in discerning our way through life's labyrinth, offering women, from entrepreneurs to seekers, a means to navigate with confidence and clarity.

Intuition is our internal compass, a treasure that, when embraced, guides us towards decisions that resonate with our deepest truths. By cultivating a connection to this intuitive wisdom, we open ourselves to a source of clarity that transcends conventional reasoning, lighting our way through both personal challenges and professional crossroads.

In this exploration, we dismantle the myths that cloud the nature of intuition, celebrating it as an accessible, universal gift. Through techniques like meditation and mindful reflection, we enhance our receptivity to intuitive insights, learning to trust the guidance that arises from within.

Additionally, this chapter highlights the symbiotic relationship between self-awareness and intuitive clarity. By nurturing an understanding of our core values and desires, we amplify the voice of our intuition, enabling it to guide us with greater precision.

"Finding Direction with Intuitive Insight" is not just an exploration but an invitation to trust in the power of our inner wisdom. It equips us with the tools and confidence needed to navigate life's mazes, inspired by the knowledge that our intuition is a steadfast guide towards fulfillment and success.

# Chapter 11 Quests

### *Affirmations To Help Make It Through Tough Times*

In times of uncertainty and challenge, trusting your intuition can be a powerful tool for navigating through the turmoil. Here are some powerful affirmations designed to help strengthen your trust in your intuition and guide you toward inner peace and clarity.

I trust the wisdom that resides within me.

My intuition is a guiding light, showing me the way through the darkness.

I am attuned to the subtle signals from my inner self.

Every moment, my intuition grows stronger and clearer.

I listen with an open heart and mind to my intuitive insights.

My intuition leads me towards paths of healing and growth.

I honor my feelings and instincts as messengers of truth.

In quiet moments, my intuition speaks to me with clarity and purpose.

I am deeply connected to my inner wisdom, guiding me in every decision.

I trust my intuition to reveal what is unseen and to guide me in the right direction.

My inner voice is a trusted advisor, and I listen to its counsel with confidence.

I allow my intuition to lead me, knowing it understands my highest good.

Every day, in every way, my intuitive powers are expanding.

I am open to receiving intuitive guidance in all aspects of my life.

My intuition is a compass that never steers me wrong.

I trust the process of intuitive decision-making.

I give myself permission to follow my intuition without fear.

My intuition is a sacred gift, and I use it with gratitude and wisdom.

I am intuitively guided to solutions and opportunities.

Trusting my intuition brings me peace of mind and heart.

I am surrounded by the protective energy of my intuition, guiding me through troubled times.

Repeating these affirmations can help to reinforce your connection to your intuition, especially during moments of doubt or difficulty. Trusting this inner guidance system can lead to a more aligned, authentic, and fulfilling life journey.

## *Embracing Your Fate*

Sage Philosopher Friedrich Nietzsche's concept of "embracing your fate" is most closely associated with the idea of "amor fati," which is Latin for "love of one's fate." Nietzsche uses this term to express the idea that one should not only accept but also love everything that happens in life, seeing it as necessary and valuable to the overall fabric of one's existence. That means no cherry picking only those circumstances that you like but also the hard times that appear on life's roadmap.

This concept is found in various writings of Nietzsche, but it is most explicitly discussed in "Ecce Homo: How One Becomes What One Is," which is an autobiographical work where Nietzsche reflects on his own life and philosophy. In it, he states:

"My formula for greatness in a human being is amor fati: that one wants nothing to be different, not forward, not backward, not in all eternity. Not merely bear what is necessary, still less conceal it—all idealism is mendacity in the face of what is necessary—but love it."

Nietzsche's emphasis on amor fati is not a call to passivity or resignation but rather an encouragement to embrace life's challenges, to find joy and purpose in the struggle, and to perceive the beauty in the necessity of every moment and event. By loving one's fate, Nietzsche believed that individuals could achieve a profound sense of freedom and empowerment, transcending the vicissitudes of life through a deep acceptance and affirmation of existence as it is.

## *Common Misconceptions About Intuition*

Drawing from the wealth of information and insights into the realm of intuition and psychic abilities provided in the documents, here are several common misconceptions about intuition that have been clarified:

**Intuition is the Same for Everyone**: Intuition manifests uniquely for each individual. While some may receive intuitive insights as a gut feeling, others might experience them through dreams, sudden thoughts, or physical sensations. The diversity in how intuition presents itself underscores the importance of personal exploration and understanding of one's own intuitive language.

**Only Certain People are Intuitive**: A prevalent misconception is that intuition is a special ability reserved for a select few. However, the truth is that everyone has intuitive capabilities. Just like any skill, the strength and clarity of one's intuition can be developed over time through practice and attention.

**Intuition is Always Right**: While intuition can be a powerful guide, it is essential to recognize that it is influenced by our perceptions, emotions, and past experiences. Therefore, it may not always provide a clear or accurate direction. Balancing intuition with rational thought and considering the context can lead to more informed decisions.

**Intuition is Magical or Supernatural**: Many view intuition as a mystical or unexplainable force. Although intuition can seem magical, it is a natural part of human cognition. It arises from our subconscious mind's ability to rapidly process information and recognize patterns beyond our conscious awareness.

**Developing Intuition Requires Special Tools or Rituals**: While tools like crystals, tarot cards, and meditation can support intuitive development, they are not strictly necessary. The key to enhancing intuition lies in fostering a deep connection with oneself, regularly practicing mindfulness, and trusting one's inner voice.

**Intuition and Logic are Opposites**: Another common belief is that intuition and logic are mutually exclusive. In reality, they are complementary aspects of human cognition. Combining intuitive insights with logical analysis can lead to more holistic and effective decision-making.

**Strong Intuition Means Never Facing Challenges**: Some may assume that with a highly developed intuition, one can avoid all life's difficulties. However, challenges are a natural part of life and growth. Intuition can provide guidance and insight, but it does not grant immunity from facing obstacles.

Understanding these misconceptions can empower individuals to explore and trust their intuition more freely, recognizing it as a valuable and natural aspect of human experience. By acknowledging and working through these misconceptions, one can more fully integrate intuition into their daily life and decision-making processes.

*Chapter 12*

# LIVING AN
# INTUITIVE LIFE

### *Daily Integration of Intuition*

While it has been fifty plus years since I first began to understand what intuition was, what it felt like and what it can mean in our day to day I have never lost the excitement of my early days in learning to work with it. The relationship that you develop with your inner guidance is a relationship that, once established, will never fail you. I use it all day every day and you will be able to too.

Embarking on this journey involves first cultivating a heightened state of awareness. It is about creating moments of stillness in our day to quiet the mind and connect deeply with our inner self. Practices like mindfulness and meditation serve not just as tools for relaxation, but as gateways to attuning ourselves to the subtle intuitive nudges that often get overlooked amidst life's noise.

Trusting our intuition is another vital strand in this tapestry. It is easy to doubt those gut feelings or write them off as irrelevant, but intuition is a compass pointing towards our truth and authenticity. By valuing and acting on these inner promptings, we strengthen our trust in our own wisdom, navigating life's decisions with greater confidence and clarity.

Incorporating intuitive practices into our daily routine acts as the thread that binds this tapestry together. Whether it is through journaling, engaging in creative pursuits, or simply pausing to reflect, these activities foster a space where intuition can flourish, guiding us towards decisions and actions that resonate deeply with our core.

Moreover, embracing the journey of integrating intuition into our lives is enriched by the fellowship of like-minded individuals. Seeking out communities or mentors who cherish the intuitive process can illuminate our path with shared experiences and support, fostering an environment where growth and intuition thrive side by side.

### A Lifelong Intuitive Journey

One of the nice things about the cultivation of our intuition is that it's a lifelong journey. This sacred quest, outlined in "Awaken Your Intuition: Empowering Women for Success in Life and Business," beckons us to nurture our intuitive sense, transforming it into a constant guide through the seasons of our lives. The expressions of our inner wisdom grow as we do and adapt to our needs as maids, mothers and crones. And, unlike other things in life, intuition improves with age.

Intuition serves as a bridge to the deeper wisdom residing within us, offering insights that transcend the limitations of logical thought. It is a conversation with the soul, a connection to the universe's rhythm that guides us toward our true path. Yet, this profound ally requires our attention and care to fully manifest its potential.

This journey invites us to engage in practices that enrich the soil of our intuition. By embracing mindfulness, meditation, and self-reflection, we create a fertile ground for our intuition to grow. These practices not only enhance our sensitivity to intuitive insights but also provide a sanctuary of calm in the midst of life's storms.

As we learn to trust and act on our intuitive insights, we embark on a path of inspired action. Stories of women who have harnessed their intuition to navigate life's challenges and achieve success serve as beacons of inspiration, encouraging us to trust in the power of our inner knowing.

## The Rich Tapestry of an Intuitive Life

Intuition, our inner sage, offers a perspective that goes beyond the tangible, guiding us through life's maze with a gentle assurance. By embracing this inner wisdom, we unlock a treasure trove of insight, leading us to choices that resonate with our soul's deepest desires.

In this exploration, we unravel the profound impact intuition has on personal fulfillment and professional achievement. It is about recognizing intuition as a catalyst for joy, a key to unlocking doors to opportunities that align with our true essence, and a guide through the complexities of career and creative endeavors.

Engaging with our intuition transforms the journey into one of discovery and alignment, where every decision is infused with a sense of purpose and authenticity. This chapter is an invitation to weave intuition into the very fabric of our being, celebrating it as the cornerstone of a life lived fully and true to oneself.

By nurturing our intuitive connection, we not only navigate life's challenges with grace but also sculpt a legacy of achievement rooted in our deepest truths. This narrative offers a roadmap for those ready to embrace their intuitive power, lighting the way to a life of passion, purpose, and profound success.

# Chapter 12 Quest

## *Client Case Studies*

Over the past 40 years I have had the honor to read tens of thousands of women. Here are a few case studies of ways women use their intuition in day to day experiences to help them live their best lives. I hope they demonstrate what is possible when using our gift and inspire you to incorporate intuition in all areas of your life.

## Case Study For Leaving Corporate To Follow Your Dream

In this case study, we explore the journey of Jewel, a woman who navigated the transition from a high-pressure corporate job to founding a successful catering company, guided by her intuition and a deep desire for fulfillment. Her story is a testament to the power of listening to one's inner voice and the courage required to follow one's true path.

## Background

Nina had spent over a decade climbing the corporate ladder in a healthcare company. Despite her successful career, she felt a growing sense of disconnection from her work and a lack of purpose. Nina had always been passionate about cooking and often found solace in the kitchen, creating dishes that brought joy to her friends and family. Her intuition whispered persistently that her passion could be more than just a hobby, but fear of the unknown and the security of her corporate job held her back.

## Intuitive Awakening

The turning point came during a particularly reflective period in her life. Nina began to engage more deeply with her spiritual practice, incorporating meditation and journaling into her daily routine. Through this process, she became more attuned to her intuition, which consistently guided her towards pursuing her love for cooking as a career. Nina described experiencing a series of synchronicities that seemed to affirm her new direction, including chance encounters with successful entrepreneurs and stumbling upon a vacant kitchen space that seemed perfect for a startup catering business.

## Taking the Leap

Despite the fear and uncertainty, Nina decided to trust her intuition and take the leap. She enrolled in a culinary program to refine her skills and began to outline a business plan. Drawing upon her corporate experience, Nina approached her new venture with discipline and strategic planning, but it was her intuition that guided the ethos of her business. She focused on creating dishes that were not only delicious but also nourishing, using locally sourced and sustainable ingredients.

## Challenges and Triumphs

Nina faced numerous challenges in the early days, from financial uncertainty to learning the ropes of a new industry. However, her intuitive approach to business, which emphasized authenticity, connection, and quality, resonated with her clients. Word of mouth spread, and soon Nina's catering company became known for its unique offerings and heartfelt service.

## Success and Expansion

Over the years, Nina's company grew from a small startup to a thriving business, catering for private events, corporate functions, and community gatherings. She expanded her team, bringing on staff who shared her vision and values. Nina credits her success to the alignment between her inner values and her professional endeavors, a harmony she found by listening to her intuition.

## Key Insights

Trust Your Intuition: Nina's journey underscores the importance of listening to one's inner voice, even when it leads you down an unconventional path.

Embrace Change: Transitioning from a secure job to starting a business is fraught with uncertainty, but embracing this change can lead to fulfilling outcomes.

Align Values with Work: Success is more satisfying and sustainable when your work reflects your personal values and passions.

The Power of Reflection: Regularly engaging in reflective practices like meditation and journaling can enhance your connection to your intuition.

Persistence Through Challenges: Challenges are inevitable in any new venture, but persistence and alignment with one's deeper intuition can guide one through to success.

Nina's story is a powerful example of how tapping into our intuition can lead us to realize our passions and achieve success that resonates with our deepest selves. Her journey from the corporate world to the kitchen is not just about changing careers but about finding a path that aligns with one's soul's calling.

## Case Study On Intuition And Love

### Background

Samantha, a 34-year-old graphic designer from New Orleans, had experienced her fair share of dating mishaps and mismatches. Despite her successes in her career and a vibrant social life, Samantha felt a void when it came to romantic relationships. She had tried various dating apps, set-ups by friends, and even singles events, but none led to the meaningful connection she yearned for.

### The Turning Point

After another disappointing date, Samantha decided to take a different approach. She recalled how her intuition had guided her successfully in other areas of her life, such as her career and friendships. Wondering if the same could apply to her love life,

Samantha decided to consciously tap into her intuition to guide her search for love.

## Strategy

Samantha began her journey by dedicating time each day to meditate and reflect on what she truly desired in a partner. Instead of focusing on superficial attributes, she concentrated on how she wanted to feel in a relationship. She sought a connection that was deep, authentic, and supportive. During these moments of reflection, she asked her intuition to guide her toward finding this person.

She also decided to become more mindful in her daily life, paying attention to her feelings and hunches about the people she met. Samantha started listening more to her inner voice, trusting it to guide her actions and decisions in her social and dating life.

## Intuitive Actions

One day, while at a coffee shop, Samantha felt a strong, inexplicable urge to strike up a conversation with a stranger sitting nearby, something she would not typically do. They quickly discovered a mutual love for hiking and art, leading to an exchange of numbers. On another occasion, her intuition nudged her to attend a workshop on creative writing, a passion of hers she had neglected. There, she met several new friends who introduced her to a broader social circle, expanding her connections in meaningful ways.

## Outcome

It was not long before one of the friendships developed into something more. Alex, someone she met through the new friends from the writing workshop, shared Samantha's passion for creativity, along with a deep sense of empathy and a love for adventure. Their relationship blossomed naturally, marked by a profound understanding and respect for each other.

## Reflection

Looking back, Samantha realized that by tuning into her intuition, she not only found love but also enriched her life in unexpected ways. She learned that intuition could be a powerful guide in her search for a partner, leading her not just to any relationship, but to the right one for her.

## Conclusion

Samantha's story illustrates the transformative power of intuition in finding love. By listening to her inner voice and following its guidance, she was able to connect with someone who truly complemented her in ways she had always hoped for. This case study serves as a testament to the idea that when we align with our inner guidance, we open ourselves up to the possibilities of profound connections and love.

## Case Study: Emma's Journey to Finding Her Tribe Through Intuition

### Background

Emma, a 24-year-old graphic designer from Austin, Texas, found herself feeling isolated and disconnected after graduating from college and entering the professional world. Despite having a successful career and a loving family, she longed for a sense of belonging and community—a "tribe" with whom she could share her passions, fears, and dreams.

### Challenge

The challenge Emma faced was not uncommon: how to find genuine, like-minded individuals in a world that often feels superficial and disconnected. Traditional methods of making friends, such as networking events or social media, left her feeling even more isolated. Emma yearned for connections that were authentic and aligned with her values and interests, particularly in the realms of creativity, sustainability, and personal growth.

### Intuitive Approach

Frustrated by the lack of success in finding her community through conventional means, Emma decided to take a different approach. She turned inward, trusting that her intuition would guide her to the people and places where she would naturally belong. Emma began to pay close attention to her feelings and instincts about the environments she was in and the people she encountered.

**Key Intuitive Decisions**

1. Following Her Passions: Emma decided to engage more deeply with activities that brought her joy and fulfillment, regardless of whether she had company. She joined a local art class, attended workshops on sustainability, and participated in community garden projects. These were all areas she felt a strong intuitive pull towards.

2. Listening to Her Gut: Whenever Emma met new people, she paid close attention to her initial gut feelings. If someone's energy did not feel right, she did not force a connection. Conversely, when she felt a natural ease and excitement in someone's presence, she pursued that relationship further.

3. Creating Spaces for Connection: Emma used her skills as a graphic designer to organize a small, local exhibition of artists focused on themes of nature and sustainability. She trusted her intuition that this event would attract like-minded individuals. She also started a monthly meet-up for creative professionals looking to integrate sustainability into their work.

**Outcome**

Emma's intuitive approach led her to find a community of individuals who shared her passions and values. The art class introduced her to fellow artists who became close friends and collaborators. The sustainability workshops and community garden projects connected her with activists and thinkers who were equally passionate about making a difference in the world. Her exhibition and meet-up became popular in her local area, attracting a diverse group of creative and eco-conscious individuals.

## Reflection

Looking back, Emma realized that by following her intuition and engaging deeply with her interests, she naturally attracted people who resonated with her authentic self. She learned that finding her tribe was less about looking outward and more about honoring her inner voice and being true to herself.

# Conclusion

Emma's story is a testament to the power of intuition in finding one's community. By trusting her instincts and pursuing her passions without compromise, she was able to create meaningful connections that enriched her life immeasurably. Her journey underscores the importance of listening to one's inner guidance in the search for belonging and community.

## Case Study: Julia's Intuition-Led Success in Sustainable Fashion

## Background

Julia, a 38-year-old entrepreneur based in Manhattan, embarked on a journey to create a sustainable fashion brand that not only promoted eco-friendly practices but also empowered local artisans. With a background in fashion design and a passion for environmental conservation, Julia was determined to make a difference in the fashion industry, which is often criticized for its wasteful practices and unethical labor conditions.

## Challenge

The sustainable fashion industry is crowded and competitive, with many brands vying for the attention of a growing but discerning consumer base that values authenticity, sustainability, and ethical production. Julia faced the daunting task of distinguishing her brand in this competitive market, securing funding, and building a supply chain that was truly sustainable and ethical.

## Intuition as a Strategy

From the outset, Julia decided to rely heavily on her intuition to guide her business decisions. This approach was unconventional in the data-driven world of entrepreneurship, but Julia believed that her intuitive understanding of her target market and her deep passion for sustainability would lead her to success.

## Key Intuitive Decisions

1. Choosing Artisans Over Factories: Early in her venture, Julia felt a strong gut feeling that she should partner with local artisans rather than going the traditional route of manufacturing in overseas factories. This decision was risky due to higher costs and potentially lower production rates, but Julia's intuition told her that the story and quality of artisan-made products would resonate deeply with her audience.

2. Launching a Crowdfunding Campaign: Despite advice to seek traditional investment, Julia felt a compelling pull to launch a crowdfunding campaign. She believed that this approach would not only raise the necessary funds but also build a community of

supporters who were invested in the brand's mission from the start. Her intuition proved correct, as the campaign exceeded its funding goal and created a buzz around her brand.

3. Product Line Expansion Decision: When considering expanding her product line, Julia experienced a strong intuitive nudge to focus on a range of eco-friendly accessories made from recycled materials, even though market research suggested that apparel had higher demand. This decision paid off when the accessories line garnered significant media attention and became a best-seller, setting her brand apart in the crowded market.

**Outcome**

Julia's intuition-led approach to business led to significant successes:

Brand Differentiation: By focusing on local artisans and sustainable practices, Julia's brand carved out a unique niche in the sustainable fashion market, attracting customers who valued the stories behind their garments.

Community Engagement: The crowdfunding campaign not only provided the necessary startup capital but also built a loyal customer base that felt a strong connection to the brand's mission and success.

Market Impact: The unexpected success of the eco-friendly accessories line demonstrated the market's appetite for innovative, sustainable products and solidified Julia's brand as a leader in sustainable fashion innovation.

## Reflection

Julia's success story highlights the power of intuition in entrepreneurship. By listening to her inner voice and aligning her business decisions with her values and passions, Julia was able to navigate the complexities of the fashion industry and create a brand that stood for something meaningful. Her journey underscores the importance of trusting one's intuition, especially when it guides you toward decisions that challenge conventional wisdom but feel deeply right on a personal level.

## Conclusion

This case study illustrates that intuition can be an entrepreneur's greatest asset. Julia's intuitive approach enabled her to make bold decisions that not only differentiated her brand but also contributed to its commercial and ethical success. Her story serves as an inspiration for other entrepreneurs to consider the value of their intuition in guiding their business strategies.

## Case Study: Sophia's Creative Awakening

## Introduction

Sophia, a 28-year-old entrepreneur from San Francisco, embarked on a journey that transformed not only her startup but also her personal understanding of creativity and inspiration. As the founder of an innovative tech company focused on sustainable solutions, Sophia faced the usual challenges of stagnation and burnout. However, her unique approach to overcoming these hurdles provides valuable insights into the power of connecting with one's creative muse for success.

## Background

Sophia's company, a Greentech consulting firm, had shown promising early growth. Yet, as the demands of running a startup increased, Sophia found herself struggling to maintain the same level of creativity and enthusiasm that initially fueled her venture. Despite her hard work and dedication, she felt disconnected from the innovative spark that had once driven her.

## The Turning Point

Realizing that traditional methods of problem-solving and brainstorming were not yielding the desired results, Sophia decided to explore alternative approaches to reignite her creativity. She began with a retreat to a quiet, nature-rich environment, away from the hustle and bustle of Silicon Valley. It was here that Sophia embarked on a guided visualization practice designed to connect individuals with their creative muse.

## Connecting with the Creative Muse

During the visualization, Sophia imagined herself in a serene forest, where she encountered a figure that embodied her creative muse. This figure, a representation of her innermost creative spirit, communicated with Sophia through vivid imagery and emotions, offering her guidance and inspiration. The experience was profoundly impactful, leaving Sophia with a renewed sense of purpose and a wealth of innovative ideas.

## Implementing Creative Insights

Sophia returned to her company with a new approach to problem-solving and product development. She instituted regular "creative sessions" for her team, where conventional thinking was set aside in favor of more intuitive, imaginative methods. Sophia encouraged her team to engage in their own practices of connecting with their creativity, fostering an environment where innovation thrived.

## Outcomes

The results were remarkable. Greentech Innovations experienced a surge in productivity and innovation. The company successfully launched a groundbreaking sustainable product that set new standards in the industry. Sophia's leadership and her commitment to nurturing creativity within her team were widely recognized, earning her and her company several prestigious awards.

## Reflection

Sophia's journey highlights the transformative power of connecting with one's creative muse. By stepping away from traditional frameworks and embracing her inner source of inspiration, Sophia not only revitalized her business but also set a precedent for how creativity can be harnessed for success in the entrepreneurial world.

## Conclusion

Sophia's case study serves as an inspiring example for entrepreneurs and creatives alike. It demonstrates that accessing and nurturing one's creative muse can lead to unprecedented levels of success and innovation. Sophia's experience underscores the importance of looking inward for inspiration and illustrates the boundless potential that lies within the realm of creative exploration.

## Case Study: Intuitive Leadership in IT Project Management

## Background

The subject of this case study is Maria, a seasoned Project Manager with over a decade of experience in the Information Technology (IT) sector. Sarah is known among her peers and team members for her exceptional technical skills, strong work ethic, and notably, her intuitive approach to leadership and project management. This study explores how Maria's intuition has played a pivotal role in her leadership style, contributing to her team's success and the overall positive outcome of her projects.

## The Scenario

Maria was leading a complex software development project aimed at creating a new customer relationship management (CRM) system for a large, multinational corporation. The project had a tight deadline, a limited budget, and high expectations for innovation and efficiency improvements. The team consisted of highly skilled professionals, but the project was falling behind schedule due to unforeseen technical challenges and team dynamics issues.

## Intuitive Intervention

While Maria's training and experience provided her with a solid foundation in traditional project management methodologies, it was her intuition that led to a breakthrough in the project. She noticed subtle signs of stress and dissatisfaction among her team members, which were not evident in the project's metrics or reports. Trusting her gut feeling, Maria decided to conduct one-on-one meetings with each team member to understand their concerns, challenges, and suggestions for the project.

These conversations revealed that while the team was technically competent, there was a lack of clear communication and collaboration, leading to inefficiencies and frustration. Additionally, Maria's intuition guided her to identify that the existing project management tools and techniques were not fully aligned with the team's needs and the project's unique challenges.

## Strategic Changes

Based on her intuitive insights, Maria implemented several strategic changes to the project management approach:

1. Enhanced Communication: Maria introduced daily stand-up meetings to facilitate better communication and collaboration among team members. These meetings provided a platform for team members to share updates, challenges, and solutions in a timely and efficient manner.

2. Flexible Methodologies: Recognizing the limitations of the current project management methodology, Maria integrated aspects of

Agile methodologies into the project's approach. This allowed for more flexibility, quicker iterations, and a greater focus on delivering value to the client.

3. Empowered Team Members: Maria encouraged team members to take ownership of their tasks and contribute ideas for improving project outcomes. By fostering an environment of trust and empowerment, Maria was able to leverage the diverse skills and creativity of her team.

**Outcomes**

The changes implemented by Maria led to a significant turnaround in the project. The team's morale improved, and there was a noticeable increase in productivity and collaboration. The project was completed on time, within budget, and exceeded the client's expectations in terms of innovation and efficiency.

**Conclusion**

Maria's case highlights the importance of intuition in IT project management. While technical skills and traditional methodologies are crucial, the ability to sense underlying issues and dynamics can lead to more effective leadership and project outcomes. Maria's intuitive approach allowed her to navigate complex challenges, foster a positive team environment, and lead her project to success, demonstrating that intuition can be a powerful tool in the arsenal of a project manager.

## Case Study: Enhancing Intuition Through Meditation in Personal Development

### Background

Linda is a 45-year-old professional working in a high-stress corporate environment. She has always been interested in personal development and the power of intuition in making life and career decisions. However, Linda found that the constant pressure and noise of her daily environment were dampening her intuitive senses. Seeking a way to reconnect with her inner voice and enhance her intuition, Linda turned to meditation.

### Objective

Linda's primary objective was to increase her intuition to better navigate her personal and professional life. She hoped that by strengthening her intuitive abilities, she would be able to make more aligned and effective decisions, reduce stress, and achieve a greater sense of fulfillment.

### Method

Linda embarked on a journey of meditation with the following structured approach:

1. Daily Practice: She committed to meditating for 20 minutes every morning before starting her day. Linda chose a quiet spot in her home where she would not be disturbed.

2. Focused Intentions: Before each session, Linda set an intention to open herself up to her intuitive insights, asking for clarity and guidance on specific questions or decisions she faced.

3. Mindfulness Meditation: Linda practiced mindfulness meditation, focusing on her breath and observing her thoughts and feelings without judgment. This practice helped her develop a deeper awareness of her inner state.

4. Journaling: After each meditation session, Linda journaled her experiences, noting any feelings, thoughts, or intuitive insights that arose during her practice.

5. Reflection and Application: Linda dedicated time each week to reflect on her journal entries and the intuitive insights she received. She then considered how these insights could be applied to her decision-making processes in her personal and professional life.

**Outcomes**

After six months of consistent meditation practice, Linda reported significant improvements in her intuitive abilities and overall well-being:

Increased Intuition: Linda noticed a marked increase in her intuitive insights, often experiencing clear guidance on decisions where she previously felt unsure. She found herself trusting these insights more, leading to more confident decision-making.

Reduced Stress Levels: Meditation helped Linda manage her stress more effectively. She felt more centered and less reactive to the pressures of her work environment, contributing to an overall sense of calm and well-being.

Improved Decision Making: By tapping into her intuition, Linda made several key decisions that positively impacted her career and personal life. She reported feeling more aligned with her true desires and values, leading to greater satisfaction and success in her endeavors.

Enhanced Self-awareness: The practice of mindfulness and journaling increased Linda's self-awareness, allowing her to understand her thought patterns, emotional triggers, and the deeper reasons behind her decisions.

## Conclusion

Linda's case demonstrates the profound impact that meditation can have on enhancing intuition. Through her dedicated practice, she was able to quiet the external noise and connect with her inner guidance, leading to improved decision-making, reduced stress, and a more fulfilling life. This case study underscores the potential of meditation as a powerful tool for personal and professional development, particularly for those seeking to harness the power of their intuition.

*Conclusion*

# NURTURING THE LIGHT OF INTUITION

C ongratulations, radiant beings, on embarking upon an enchanting journey of self-discovery and empowerment, delving deep into the essence of your intuition with "Awaken Your Intuition: Empowering Women for Success in Life and Business." Together, we have journeyed across the vast landscape of your inner universe, unveiling the hidden jewels of wisdom that patiently waited to be acknowledged and celebrated.

To every brilliant woman, seeker, visionary, and architect of the future, the pathway to success is intricately laced with the golden threads of self-awareness and the mystical practice of intuition. Throughout this expedition, you have answered the call to cultivate your intuitive essence, to heed the advice of your inner sage, and to forge pathways that resonate with the true melody of your soul.

This exploration has lifted the veil to reveal a realm where doubts fade into the background, allowing you to step into a space of clarity and trust in your unique voice, shedding the layers that sought validation from the world. You have learned the art of moving in harmony with your soul's whispers, guiding you towards choices that illuminate your path with potential and alignment.

The journey has illuminated the universal truth that intuition is not a hidden secret reserved for a select few but a vibrant light within us all. By honing this sacred connection, you have accessed a wellspring of insight, enriching your personal growth and professional journey.

We have meandered through a labyrinth of practices that elevate your intuitive voice, from the serenity of meditation and the depth of mindfulness to the introspective world of journaling and the insightful realm of dream interpretation. These paths have invited you to quiet the external noise and tune into the profound guidance within.

Remember, awakening your intuition is a continuous voyage, not a destination. As you navigate forward, let the beacon of your intuitive light shine ever brighter. Cultivate this divine link through ongoing self-care, mindfulness, and the fellowship of kindred spirits who resonate with your journey.

Embraced by your intuition, you will find the universe aligning in your favor, opening doors and lighting your way with purpose and joy. Trust in this sacred journey, believe in your boundless potential, and celebrate the power nestled within your being.

With the wisdom and practices to guide you by the stars of your intuition, you are set to reach new heights. Embrace the journey, savor the victories, and unfold into the most luminous version of yourself. The adventure of intuitive living is just beginning, and the horizon is rich with endless possibilities.

May your intuition serve as the compass guiding you to a life filled with success, bliss, and profound satisfaction. Stand proud, for you are a lighthouse of hope, and with the compass of intuition in your grasp, no ocean is too vast to cross.

March on, empowered souls, seekers of the light, creators of dreams, and pioneers of new paths, letting the brilliance of your intuition reveal a world where your aspirations take wing and soar into the realms of the extraordinary.

*Lagniappe*

# A LITTLE
# SOMETHING
# EXTRA

Here in New Orleans we have an idea of something called Lagniappe which translates to A Little Something Extra. An example is if you buy something we just naturally increase it's value by giving more than what you paid for. Here are just a few goodies I wanted to share to help further cement your relationship with your intuition and to say thank you for joining me on this journey. I am so excited for your journey now that you have done the work to Awaken Your Intuition. May you always be guided by grace and love in all the ways you incorporate it into your daily lives.

## Recommended Reading

"The Intuition of the Will" (1908) by James Ward - An exploration of intuition as it relates to will and consciousness, offering early philosophical insights into the nature of intuitive processes.

"Mysticism" (1911) by Evelyn Underhill - This classic study provides a comprehensive look at mysticism, where intuition plays a central role in experiencing the divine or ultimate reality.

"The Wisdom of the Unconscious" (1940) by Carl Jung - Jung's works delve into the depths of the unconscious mind, where he believes the roots of intuition lie, offering a psychological perspective on intuition.

"An Experiment with Time" (1927) by J.W. Dunne- Dunne explores precognitive dreams and the nonlinear nature of time, suggesting that intuition can bridge past, present, and future.

"The Creative Process" (1952) by Brewster Ghiselli - A compilation of essays by various thinkers and artists, shedding light on intuition's role in creativity and innovation.

"The Tao of Physics" (1975) by Fritjof Capra - Capra draws parallels between modern physics and Eastern mysticism, highlighting intuitive understanding in the exploration of the universe.

"The Intuitive Way: The Definitive Guide to Increasing Your Awareness" by Penney Peirce - This book offers a comprehensive approach to developing intuition, combining insightful exercises with deep philosophical discussions on the nature of intuition.

"Practical Intuition" by Laura Day - Laura Day presents intuition as a practical skill that can be developed and applied in daily life, providing exercises that encourage readers to trust and act on their intuitive insights.

"Trust Your Vibes: Secret Tools for Six-Sensory Living" by Sonia Choquette - Choquette's work is a guide to living a more intuitive, spirit-guided life. She provides practical advice on how to listen to your inner voice and improve your intuitive abilities.

"The Gift of Intuition: Guiding Your Life with Love and Wisdom" by Judith Orloff- Dr. Orloff combines her insights as a psychiatrist with her personal experiences and intuitive gifts, offering strategies to recognize and honor your intuition for a more fulfilling life.

"Intuition: Knowing Beyond Logic" by Osho - Osho explores the concept of intuition as a higher form of intelligence beyond the confines of logical reasoning, offering perspectives on how to access and cultivate this inner wisdom.

"Blink: The Power of Thinking Without Thinking" by Malcolm Gladwell - Gladwell examines the power and process of intuitive thought, illustrating through examples how our best decisions are often those made instinctively, in the blink of an eye.

"Intuitive Being: Connect with Spirit, Find Your Center, and Choose an Intentional Life" by Jill Willard- Willard presents intuition as a key to living a balanced and intentional life, offering insights into how to align with your true self through intuitive practices.

"The Third Eye" by Sophia Stewart - Though more esoteric, this book delves into the concept of the third eye as an intuitive and spiritual guide, offering a unique perspective on accessing and enhancing psychic abilities.

"Psychic Development for Beginners: An Easy Guide to Developing & Releasing Your Psychic Abilities" by William W. Hewitt - This book provides a practical approach to developing psychic abilities, emphasizing intuition as a key component of psychic development

"Awakening Intuition" by Mona Lisa Schulz - Schulz combines her medical background with intuitive practice, offering a guide to using intuition to enhance health, well-being, and personal growth.

"The Science of Intuition: How to Access the Inner-net of Intuitive Knowledge" by Mona Lisa Schulz - A follow-up to her earlier work, Schulz dives deeper into the scientific underpinnings of intuition, providing a robust framework for understanding and harnessing this powerful inner resource.

"Drawing on the Right Side of the Brain" (1979) by Betty Edwards - Although focused on drawing, this book is fundamentally about accessing and developing the intuitive, right-brain capabilities.

"The Artist's Way" (1992) by Julia Cameron - Cameron's book is a seminal work in creativity and personal development, advocating for the use of intuition in the artistic process and beyond intuition works in various contexts.

"The Field: The Quest for the Secret Force of the Universe" (2002) by Lynne McTaggart - McTaggart explores scientific studies that suggest the existence of a connecting field of energy, which could be foundational to understanding intuition.

"Intuition Pumps and Other Tools for Thinking" (2013) by Daniel Dennett- Dennett presents various thought experiments and methodologies to enhance thinking and, indirectly, intuitive insights.

"The Gift of Fear: Survival Signals That Protect Us from Violence" by Gavin de Becker - A compelling look at how intuition can be a powerful tool in recognizing and avoiding danger.

"The Seat of the Soul" by Gary Zukav- This book delves into the connection between intuition and the soul, offering insights into how intuition can lead to spiritual growth and alignment.

"Intuitive Being: Connect with Spirit, Find Your Center, and Choose an Intentional Life" by Jill Willard** - Willard shares her insights on how to balance energy, live in harmony with intuition, and connect with one's higher self.

"Developing Intuition: Practical Guidance for Daily Life" by Shakti Gawain - Gawain offers simple, yet effective practices to help readers listen to their inner voice and use intuition as a guide in making life choices.

"Intuition at Work: Why Developing Your Gut Instincts Will Make You Better at What You Do" by Gary Klein- Klein demonstrates the value of intuition in professional settings and offers strategies for developing intuitive skills in the workplace.

"Big Magic: Creative Living Beyond Fear" by Elizabeth Gilbert - Gilbert explores the mysterious nature of inspiration and creativity, encouraging readers to embrace intuition as a source of guidance and innovation.

"The Power of Your Subconscious Mind" by Joseph Murphy - Murphy provides insight into how the subconscious mind works and how to influence it through the power of thought and belief.

"The Art of Intuition: Cultivating Your Inner Wisdom" by Sophy Burnham- Burnham takes readers on a journey through history, art, and science to explore the multifaceted aspects of intuition.

"The Wise Heart: A Guide to the Universal Teachings of Buddhist Psychology" by Jack Kornfield - Kornfield introduces Buddhist psychological principles that can help cultivate intuition, compassion, and emotional healing.

"How We Decide" by Jonah Lehrer- Lehrer delves into the neuroscience behind decision-making, offering insights into how intuition plays a crucial role in our choices.

This collection aims to cater to a broad spectrum of interests and approaches, recognizing that intuition can be nurtured through various paths—be it through self-reflection, spiritual practice, creative expression, or understanding the science behind it. Each book invites readers to explore and expand their intuitive capacities, paving the way for a more attuned and insightful way of living.

## *Types OF Divination*

Divination is the practice of seeking knowledge of the future or the unknown by supernatural means. There are many different styles of divination, each with its own unique methods and meanings. Here is a list of some of the most widely recognized forms of divination and a brief description of their meanings and how they are practiced:

### Tarot Reading

Tarot reading involves the use of a deck of tarot cards to gain insight into the past, present, or future. Each card has symbolic imagery and a specific meaning that can vary depending on its position and the cards around it.

### Astrology

Astrology is the study of the movements and relative positions of celestial bodies interpreted as having an influence on human affairs and the natural world. It involves creating horoscopes based on the time, date, and place of one's birth to predict aspects of their personality and life events.

### Runes

Runes are letters from ancient alphabets, primarily used by the Norse, which are cast or drawn to gain insight into situations or questions. Each rune has a specific meaning and is interpreted based on its orientation and the context of the question.

## Palmistry

Palmistry, or chiromancy, involves reading the lines and features of the hands, particularly the palms, to interpret personality traits and predict future happenings. Each line (e.g., heart line, life line) is believed to offer different insights.

## I Ching

The I Ching, or Book of Changes, is an ancient Chinese divination text and the oldest of the Chinese classics. It involves throwing coins or yarrow stalks to form hexagrams, which are then interpreted according to the text to provide guidance.

## Numerology

Numerology is the belief in the divine or mystical relationship between numbers and coinciding events. It involves analyzing numbers, such as the date of birth, to determine a person's personality, strengths, weaknesses, and life path.

## Scrying

Scrying involves looking into a suitable medium, such as a crystal ball, water, or mirror, in the hope of detecting significant messages or visions. The images seen are interpreted symbolically.

## Tea Leaf Reading (Tasseography)

This method involves interpreting patterns in tea leaves, coffee grounds, or wine sediments to predict the future. The symbols seen in the remnants of a cup are interpreted based on traditional meanings.

## Ouija Board

The Ouija board is a flat board marked with letters, numbers, and other symbols, theoretically used to communicate with spirits. Participants place their fingers on a planchette to spell out messages during a séance.

## Pendulum Dowsing

Pendulum dowsing involves using a weighted object on a string or chain to answer questions or locate objects. The direction of its swing is interpreted as a response to questions posed by the user.

## Geomancy

Geomancy is a method of divination that interprets markings on the ground or patterns formed by tossed handfuls of soil, rocks, or sand. The modern practice often involves drawing dots on paper.

## Aura Reading

Aura reading involves interpreting a person's aura, which is believed to be a luminous energy field surrounding individuals. Readers claim to see or sense this aura and interpret its colors and patterns to determine the person's emotional, spiritual, and physical well-being.

## Bibliomancy

Bibliomancy involves using books in divination. A book is chosen as a source of truth, and questions are posed before randomly opening the book to find guidance. The Bible was historically a common choice for this practice.

These different forms of divination have been practiced across different cultures and periods, each with its own set of beliefs and methodologies. The effectiveness and belief in these practices vary widely among individuals and cultures. I have used them all and more during my training and know each to be effective. These tools can often help facilitate your connection to your intuitive sense and are good ways to begin using your intuition for others.

## *Test: Discovering Your Clair Senses*

This test is designed to help you explore whether you have tendencies towards clairvoyance (clear seeing), clairaudience (clear hearing), or clairsentience (clear feeling). Answer the following questions honestly and tally your scores to uncover your dominant clair sense.

### Instructions

For each question, choose the option that best describes your experiences or preferences. At the end, count how many As, Bs, and Cs you have to see which clair sense might be most prominent in you.

### Questions

1. When you imagine or remember a scene, how do you experience it?

A) I vividly see images, colors, or pictures in my mind.

B) I hear sounds, voices, or music in my mind.

C) I feel emotions or physical sensations.

2. When you think about a loved one, what happens first?

A) I see their face or other visual memories.

B) I hear their voice or laughter.

C) I feel the warmth, love, or comfort they bring.

3. How do you usually receive intuitive information?

A) Through spontaneous images or symbols in my mind.

B) Through words, names, or auditory information that comes to me.

C) Through gut feelings or physical sensations.

4. When you are in a new place, what do you notice first?

A) The appearance, colors, or layout.

B) The sounds, background noise, or the silence.

C) The atmosphere, vibes, or energy.

5. How do you prefer to learn new information?

A) By reading or seeing demonstrations.

B) By listening to lectures or audio recordings.

C) Through hands-on experience or by feeling it out.

6. When you think about the future, how do you envision it?

A) I picture potential scenarios or visual outcomes.

B) I think about conversations or messages that could occur.

C) I have a sense of hope, worry, or anticipation, but it is more a feeling than an image or sound.

7. When you receive guidance or an important insight, it usually comes to you as:

A) A clear image or sequence of images.

B) A voice, sound, or piece of music.

C) A strong feeling, sensation, or knowing.

## Scoring

Mostly As: You may have a tendency towards **Clairvoyance**. This means you are likely to receive intuitive information through visual means, such as seeing images, colors, symbols, or visions in your mind's eye.

Mostly Bs: Your dominant clair sense might be **Clairaudience**. This suggests you are prone to hearing intuitive information, which could manifest as hearing words, names, sounds, or music, even when no physical source is present.

Mostly Cs: You might be primarily **Clairsentient**. This indicates that your intuition comes through feelings, physical sensations, or emotions. You are sensitive to the energy of places, people, and situations, often "just knowing" information without knowing how.

Remember, it's possible to have abilities in more than one clair sense, and these can develop or change over time with practice and openness. This test is a starting point for exploring your intuitive gifts.

# 7 Quick Steps To Fast Track Your Intuition In Business

Intuition is a critical skill in business, offering insights that logic and data can sometimes miss. For women in business, honing intuition can be particularly powerful, blending innate sensitivities with strategic thinking. Here are seven exercises designed to develop intuition for success in the business world:

## 1. Mindful Listening Exercise

Objective: Improve your ability to listen to your inner voice and the subtle cues in business environments.

Exercise: Begin each day with a five-minute silent meditation, focusing solely on your breath. Throughout the day, practice active listening in every conversation and meeting, giving full attention without planning your response. Note any intuitive feelings or hunches that arise. Reflect on these insights at the end of the day to see how they could inform your business decisions.

## 2. Intuition Journal

Objective: Track and validate your intuitive insights to build trust in your intuition over time.

Exercise: Keep a journal dedicated to recording intuitive insights related to your business. Note the context, the intuition you had, any action you took based on it, and the outcome. Review this journal periodically to identify patterns and validate the accuracy of your intuitive decisions.

### 3. Decision-Making Reflection

Objective: Develop a deeper understanding of how your intuition influences your decision-making process.

Exercise: When faced with a decision, take a moment to quiet your mind and ask yourself what your gut feeling is about each option. Write these feelings down and then proceed with your analytical decision-making process. Compare your intuitive insights with your logical conclusions and track which decisions lead to successful outcomes.

### 4. Sensory Deprivation for Clarity

Objective: Use sensory deprivation to quiet external noise and enhance internal clarity.

-Exercise: Spend time in a quiet, darkened room, or use noise-canceling headphones to block out external sounds. Allow yourself to focus inwardly without the usual distractions. Use this time to ponder a business question or challenge, and pay attention to the insights that surface.

### 5. The Future Letter

Objective: Utilize visualization and intuition to project future business successes.

-Exercise: Write a letter to yourself from the future, describing in detail where you see your business and yourself as a leader. Focus on the feelings and intuitions that guide your actions in this future scenario. Reflect on what intuitive steps you might need to take now to make this future a reality.

## 6. Intuitive Networking

Objective: Strengthen intuitive skills in choosing business contacts and opportunities to pursue.

-Exercise: At networking events or when meeting new business contacts, tune into your initial gut reactions to people or ideas. Later, reflect on these intuitions and explore any connections or opportunities you felt particularly drawn to, even if you are not sure why. Follow up on these intuitive leads to see where they might lead.

## 7. Creative Visualization

Objective: Enhance intuition through the power of creative visualization, focusing on business goals and challenges.

Exercise: Set aside time each week to practice creative visualization. Visualize yourself successfully navigating a current business challenge or achieving a goal. Focus on the sensations, emotions, and intuition associated with this success. Afterwards, journal any intuitive insights or new ideas that came to you during the visualization.

Developing intuition can be a game-changer for women in business, providing an edge in decision-making, leadership, and navigating complex situations. Here are seven exercises specifically designed to help women harness and hone their intuitive skills for success in the business world.

## *Angel Number Meanings*

As a professional psychic, medium, and astrologer, I have come to learn that the universe has a peculiar way of communicating with us, especially through numbers. Angel numbers, those repetitive numerical sequences that keep popping up in our daily lives, are one such way. They are like a cosmic nudge, a whisper from the universe, or a gentle tap on the shoulder from our guardian angels. So, let me take you on a journey through the meanings of all eleven angel numbers, wrapping each insight in the warmth and positivity that I so love to share.

**Angel Number 111:** The Initiation

Imagine you are lighting a candle in the dark. That first flicker of flame is akin to seeing 111. It's a powerful number of manifestation, urging you to pay attention to your thoughts and intentions. The universe is saying, "Hey, you're creating what you're thinking right now, so make it positive." It is a reminder that your thoughts are potent seeds and you are the gardener.

**Angel Number 222**: Balance and Harmony

When 222 dances into your life, think of it as a cosmic pause button, urging you to take a breath and find balance. It is a reminder that you are on the right path and need to trust in the process. Whether it is in love, work, or personal growth, 222 tells you to keep the faith and stay committed to your vision.

**Angel Number 333**: The Divine Encouragement

Seeing 333 is like receiving a warm, reassuring hug from the Universe. It signifies the presence of ascended masters and guides, offering support and encouragement. It is a call to acknowledge your inner divinity and creative energies. The universe is cheering you on, saying, "Go on, darling, you've got this!"

**Angel Number 444**: Protection and Support

444 is the universe's way of saying, "I've got your back." It symbolizes protection and encouragement, reminding you that you are loved and supported by the universe and your spiritual guides. When 444 appears, know that you are surrounded by an invisible support system, ready to help you overcome any obstacle.

**Angel Number 555:** A Time for Change

Hold onto your hat because 555 signals change is coming! It is a vibrant, dynamic energy urging you to embrace the new. This number is all about personal freedom and growth, reminding you that change is not just okay; it is necessary for your soul's evolution. So, when 555 appears, get ready to say "hello" to new adventures.

**Angel Number 666:** Seek Balance and Harmony

Now, before you get spooked, 666 is not about bad omens. In the angelic realm, it is a gentle nudge to check in with yourself and find harmony. It is about balancing material desires with spiritual growth, reminding you to align your actions with your higher purpose. So, when 666 appears, it is time for a spiritual inventory.

**Angel Number 777**: Spiritual Awakening

Seeing 777 is like finding a rare treasure. It signifies spiritual enlightenment and awakening, a reminder that you are on the right spiritual path. It is an encouragement to keep going, to deepen your spiritual practices, and to trust in the magic of the universe. When 777 appears, know that you are tapping into the highest wisdom.

**Angel Number 888:** Abundance and Prosperity

When 888 pops up, get ready to open the door to abundance. This number is a sign of impending financial or personal prosperity. It is a reminder that as you give, so shall you receive. The universe is abundant, and 888 is a signal that you are aligning with that abundance. So, when you see 888, prosperity is on its way.

**Angel Number 999**: Completion and Release

999 is the closing of a chapter. It signifies completion, signaling that it is time to let go of what no longer serves you and make way for new beginnings. It is an invitation to reflect, release, and rejuvenate. When 999 appears, it is time to wrap up loose ends and prepare for a fresh start.

**Angel Number 000**: Infinite Potential

Seeing 000 is like standing at the brink of eternity, gazing into the infinite potential of the universe. It is a reminder of the endless possibilities that lie ahead and the ongoing cycles of life. When 000 appears, it is a call to connect with the divine and remember that you are a part of this magnificent universe.

**Angel Number 1010**: Spiritual Growth and Enlightenment

Lastly, 1010 is a powerful symbol of spiritual development and enlightenment. It encourages you to trust in the divine and your intuition. Seeing 1010 is a reminder that the universe is guiding you towards your highest good, urging you to stay positive and focused on your spiritual journey.

In the tapestry of life, these angel numbers are the threads that add color and depth, guiding us, comforting us, and reminding us of our connection to the divine. As you walk through the streets of New Orleans, or anywhere else in the world, keep your eyes open for these divine messages. They are a reminder that the universe speaks to those who are willing to listen, and what a beautiful conversation it is.

## *More Affirmations For Intuitive Growth And Power*

I trust my intuition to guide me to unparalleled success in my career, leading me to my true purpose and fulfillment.

My inner wisdom naturally attracts loving, supportive relationships that enrich my life and nurture my soul.

I am deeply connected to my intuitive power, allowing me to create harmony and balance within my family dynamics.

My intuition is a powerful ally in my financial decisions, guiding me towards abundance and prosperity with ease and grace.

I listen to the whispers of my body, trusting my intuition to lead me towards optimal health and well-being.

In every decision I face, I allow my intuition to light the path, ensuring each step I take is aligned with my highest good.

My intuition empowers me to embrace change, turning challenges into opportunities for growth in all areas of my life.

I am intuitively guided to make choices that enhance my energy, well-being, and spiritual growth.

My inner voice is a beacon of wisdom, guiding me towards authentic connections and true love.

I trust my intuitive insights to navigate the complexities of my career, making impactful decisions with confidence and clarity.

I embrace my intuition as a sacred tool for manifesting financial abundance, trusting in the abundance of the universe to meet my needs.

My intuition strengthens my familial bonds, guiding me to communicate with love, understanding, and empathy.

I honor my intuition by making self-care a priority, knowing that nurturing my own well-being benefits all aspects of my life.

Every day, I confidently step into my power, guided by the unwavering light of my intuition.

I trust my intuitive sense to lead me through life's uncertainties with grace, resilience, and a deep sense of peace.

My intuition is a gateway to creativity, inspiring innovative solutions in my career and personal projects.

In matters of love, I trust my intuition to discern truth from illusion, guiding me to genuine connections that uplift and inspire.

I allow my intuition to guide my financial investments and decisions, trusting that prosperity is a reflection of my inner wealth.

My intuitive guidance is a compass in the journey of parenting, leading me with wisdom and love.

I am attuned to the messages of my boy and spirit, allowing my intuition to guide me towards practices that rejuvenate and heal.

## *Simple Steps To Release Emotional Trauma And Start Healing*

Each of these practices are essential tools in your journey to living an intuitive life. Mix and match these for daily steps and incorporate them into your waking day.

**Create Quiet Time:** Dedicate a few minutes each day to sit in silence. This helps quiet the mind and makes it easier to hear your intuitive voice. Early morning or late evening can be ideal times for this practice.

**Practice Mindfulness:** Engage in mindfulness practices such as mindful breathing or walking. Pay attention to the present moment without judgment, which can enhance your ability to tune into intuitive signals.

**Keep a Journal:** Start journaling your thoughts, feelings, and any intuitive hunches you experience throughout the day. Over time, you will begin to notice patterns or recurring themes that can guide your intuition.

**Ask for Guidance:** When facing a decision, take a moment to ask your intuition for guidance. Pose a question, then let it see what insights arise spontaneously over the next hours or days.

**Trust Your Gut Feelings:** Pay attention to your body's signals. Often, intuition is felt physically, such as a gut feeling, heart flutter, or a sense of calm. Trust these feelings as valid indicators of your intuition at work.

**Meditate Regularly:** Meditation is a powerful tool for connecting with your inner self. It does not have to be lengthy; even short, daily sessions can significantly boost your intuitive abilities.

**Spend Time in Nature:** Nature has a grounding effect that can help clear your mind and open up your intuitive channels. Regular walks in a park or time spent in green spaces can facilitate this process.

**Use Reflective Questions:** When pondering a decision, ask yourself reflective questions like, "What feels right?" or "What would I choose if I wasn't afraid?" These questions can help bypass the analytical mind and tap into deeper intuition.

**Practice Decision-Making:** Give yourself permission to make small decisions based on intuition rather than over-analyzing. This could be as simple as intuitively choosing what to eat for breakfast or what color to wear. It strengthens your intuitive "muscle" through practice.

**Embrace Creativity:** Engage in creative activities without a specific goal in mind, such as doodling, writing, or playing music. Creative expression can open up intuitive pathways by bypassing the logical brain and tapping into deeper, subconscious insights.

## *Symbol Meanings*

Dreams are a reflection of our subconscious thoughts, feelings, and desires. Here is a list of the top twenty-five dream symbols and their potential meanings, offering a window into the subconscious mind:

**Water**: Represents emotions and the state of the subconscious. Calm water might indicate peace and clarity, while turbulent water can symbolize emotional turmoil.

**Teeth Falling Out:** Suggests anxiety about appearance, aging, or a sense of powerlessness.

**Being Chased:** Indicates a desire to escape from a situation or emotions you are unwilling to confront.

**Falling:** Can symbolize fear of failure, losing control, or letting go of something important.

**Flying:** Represents a desire for freedom, liberation from constraints, or an elevated perspective.

**Death:** Often signifies change, endings, and new beginnings rather than physical death.

**Taking a Test:** Reflects self-evaluation, performance anxiety, or feeling unprepared for a challenge.

**Nudity:** Suggests feelings of vulnerability, shame, or being exposed in a personal or professional situation.

**Vehicles:** Symbolize your journey through life. The condition of the vehicle may reflect your perceived control or lack thereof.

**Animals:** Can symbolize primal instincts, desires, and emotions, with the type of animal providing further insight.

**Babies:** Often signify new beginnings, innocence, or aspects of your own vulnerabilities.

**Lost or Trapped:** Reflects feelings of being stuck or unsure about your direction in life.

**Clocks**: Indicate concerns about the passage of time, deadlines, or feeling like time is running out.

**Bridges:** Symbolize transition, change, and the connection between two aspects of life or self.

**Floods:** Can represent overwhelming emotions, situations, or the need to release pent-up feelings.

**Fire:** Might symbolize passion, anger, destruction, or the need to purify and transform aspects of your life.

**School:** Often relates to lessons being learned, the pursuit of knowledge, or unresolved issues from one's schooling years.

**Mountains:** Symbolize obstacles, challenges to be overcome, or achieving high goals.

**Paths:** Reflect choices, life direction, or a journey you are on. The nature of the path can provide further insight.

**Wedding**s: Can represent commitments, transitions, or unions, not necessarily related to marriage.

**Clothing:** Often symbolizes self-expression and how you want others to perceive you.

**Phone:** Might represent communication issues or the desire to hear from someone.

**Flying Objects (UFOs, airplanes):** Can symbolize goals, aspirations, or things beyond your reach or understanding.

**Keys:** Symbolize solutions, knowledge, freedom, or opportunities.

Interpreting dream symbols is highly subjective and depends on personal experiences and emotions. These symbols can serve as a guide to understanding your subconscious thoughts and feelings. Reflecting on how they relate to your current life situations can provide meaningful insights.

**Signs That The Universe Is Trying To Get Your Attention**

**Recurring Numbers**: Seeing sequences of numbers repeatedly, like 111 or 1234, which might hold personal or universal significance.

**Synchronicities**: Experiencing meaningful coincidences that seem to offer guidance or affirm your thoughts and decisions.

**Dreams**: Having vivid dreams that provide clear messages, guidance, or reassurance about your life path.

**Intuition**: Experiencing a strong gut feeling guiding you towards or away from certain situations or decisions.

**Nature Signs**: Observing unusual patterns or occurrences in nature, such as a circle of birds or a tree that stands out to you.

**Feathers**: Finding feathers in your path, often seen as messages of love and support from deceased loved ones or angels.

**Rainbows**: Seeing rainbows, especially in unexpected situations, as signs of hope and promise.

**Butterflies or Birds**: Encountering butterflies or specific birds repeatedly, which can be interpreted as spiritual messengers.

**Lost Objects**: Finding objects that you have lost at significant moments, suggesting timing or reassurance from the universe.

**Electrical Interference**: Experiencing unusual behavior with electronics, lights flickering, or appliances malfunctioning as a form of communication.

**Music**: Hearing a particular song or piece of music at a pivotal moment, which seems to speak directly to your situation or emotions.

**Repeated Phrases or Words**: Coming across the same word, phrase, or quote multiple times in different contexts.

**Physical Sensations**: Feeling a sudden warmth, touch, or tingle, especially when thinking of a loved one or contemplating a decision.

**Seeing Specific Animals**: Encountering a specific animal or insect frequently, which might carry symbolic meaning.

**Smells**: Detecting a familiar scent with no apparent source, often associated with a deceased loved one or a memory.

**Visual Patterns**: Noticing specific symbols or patterns repeatedly, such as hearts, crosses, or circles, in various settings.

**Temperature Changes**: Feeling a sudden change in temperature, which some interpret as a spiritual presence or a sign.

**Voices or Sounds**: Hearing your name being called or specific sounds with no visible source, guiding or alerting you.

**Feeling Presence**: Sensing a presence around you, suggesting guidance or protection from a loved one or spiritual entity.

**Direct Messages**: Receiving advice, warnings, or messages that seem to come directly to your mind or through another person unexpectedly.

**Books or Articles**: Stumbling upon a book, article, or video that addresses exactly what you have been contemplating or struggling with.

**Numbers Related to Dates**: Encountering significant dates repeatedly, which might relate to birthdays, anniversaries, or historical events meaningful to you.

**Cloud Formations**: Seeing shapes or symbols in the clouds that capture your attention and seem to convey a message.

**Mirrors or Reflections**: Noticing something unusual or meaningful in a mirror or reflection that offers insight or affirmation.

**Chance Encounters**: Meeting someone by chance who offers exactly the advice, assistance, or connection you needed at that moment.

## *Intuition By The Numbers*

Compiling statistics on the use of intuition can be challenging due to the subjective nature of intuition and the variety of contexts in which it is studied. However, research across fields like psychology, business, and decision-making has yielded insights into how intuition is perceived and used. Here is a list of statistics and findings that illuminate the role of intuition in various domains:

1. Decision-Making:

A study published in the "Journal of Psychological Science" suggested that trusting one's gut feelings can lead to more accurate predictions about future events compared to using detailed analysis alone.

Research indicates that up to 90% of the critical decisions made by senior executives in large organizations may be based on gut feel or intuition (source: "Executive Intuition" by Jagdish Parikh).

2. Business and Entrepreneurship:

A survey of 1,300 senior executives across forty-four countries found that 62% of them tend to trust their gut feelings (source: a PwC global data and analytics survey).

Entrepreneurs often rely on intuition for decision-making, with some studies suggesting that over 80% of successful entrepreneurs have reported relying significantly on intuitive insight during the initial stages of their ventures.

3. Healthcare:

Among nurses, studies have shown that intuition plays a crucial role in clinical decision-making, with over 70% of experienced nurses reporting the use of intuition in their practice (source: a study in "Journal of Advanced Nursing").

A survey of general practitioners found that approximately 50% reported using intuition frequently in diagnosing patients (source: a study in "BMJ").

4. Psychology and Personal Relationships:

Research on marital satisfaction indicates that individuals who reported trusting their intuition in their initial evaluations of their partner were more likely to report higher levels of satisfaction in their marriage years later (source: a study in "Science").

A survey found that 85% of people believe they have experienced a gut feeling in relationships, with 74% saying they trust their gut feelings to make decisions in their personal lives (source: a YouGov survey).

5. Creative and Innovative Processes:

Studies on creativity and innovation suggest that intuition is a key component in the creative process, with many leading innovators and scientists reporting significant intuitive insights that led to breakthroughs.

6. Financial Decision Making:

In investment decisions, a study found that over half of the investment managers surveyed reported relying on their gut feelings to some extent, alongside analytical processes (source: a study in "The Journal of Behavioral Finance").

It's important to note that these statistics should be viewed in the context of the broader research and understanding of intuition, which highlights it as one component of decision-making. Intuition works best when used in conjunction with rational analysis, especially in complex decision-making scenarios. The effectiveness of intuition can also depend on the individual's experience, expertise, and the specific circumstances of the decision.

## *Scientific Research Into Intuition*

Research on intuition also spans various fields, including psychology, neuroscience, and decision-making studies, exploring how intuition works, its effectiveness, and its impact on behavior and choices. Below is a list of scientific studies into intuition and a summary of their findings:

1. "Intuitive and Deliberate Judgments are Based on Common Principles" by Gerd Gigerenzer (2007): This study discusses how intuition and deliberate thinking are not oppositely working processes but are based on the same principles. Gigerenzer argues that intuition can be understood as a form of unconscious intelligence that is fast and frugal.

2. "The Role of Intuitive Judgement in Mate Selection" by Martie G. Haselton and David M. Buss (2000): This research explores how intuition plays a crucial role in mate selection, suggesting that people often make rapid, intuitive judgments about potential partners based on evolutionary cues related to fertility and health.

3. "The Cognitive Reflection Test as a Predictor of Performance on Heuristics-and-Biases Tasks" by Shane Frederick (2005): Frederick's study introduces the Cognitive Reflection Test (CRT) to measure the ability or inclination to override an incorrect "gut" response and engage in further reflection. It found a correlation between CRT scores and susceptibility to biases in judgment and decision-making.

4. "Thin Slices of Expressive Behavior as Predictors of Interpersonal Consequences: A Meta-Analysis" by Nalini Ambady and Robert

Rosenthal (1992): This meta-analysis shows that brief exposures to a person's behavior (thin slices) can be used to make accurate judgments about various aspects of their personality, suggesting an intuitive ability to pick up on subtle non-verbal cues.

5. "Feeling the Future: Experimental Evidence for Anomalous Retroactive Influences on Cognition and Affect" by Daryl J. Bem (2011): Bem's controversial study suggests that humans might have the ability to feel or predict future events through processes not yet understood by science. It sparked significant debate about the nature of intuition and the methodologies for studying it.

6. "Intuition in the Context of Object Perception: Intuitive Gestalt Judgments Rest on the Unconscious Activation of Semantic Representations" by Markus Knauff et al. (2013): This study investigates how intuition in object perception works, suggesting that intuitive judgments about objects involve the unconscious activation of semantic knowledge, supporting the idea that intuition is a form of fast, unconscious cognitive processing.

7. "The Antecedents and Consequences of Intuitive Decision Making" by Gerard P. Hodgkinson et al. (2008): This research examines the factors that lead to

intuitive decision-making and its outcomes, finding that experience and expertise are critical antecedents of effective intuitive judgment.

8. "A Meta-Analytic Review of the Relationship Between Intuition and Analysis" by Jennifer S. Mueller et al. (2019): This meta-analysis reviews the complex relationship between intuitive and analytical

thinking, suggesting that while they can conflict, they often work together in decision-making processes.

9. "The Neuroscience of Intuition" by John Kounios and Mark Jung-Beeman (2009): This study explores the neural basis of intuition, identifying specific brain regions and networks involved in moments of insight or intuitive understanding, highlighting the importance of the right hemisphere in intuitive processing.

10. "Predicting Soccer Matches After Unconscious and Conscious Thought as a Function of Expertise" by Ap Dijksterhuis et al. (2009): This study compares the accuracy of soccer match predictions made after periods of unconscious thought (intuition) versus conscious deliberation, finding that experts make more accurate predictions when relying on intuition.

These studies represent a sample of the broad research into intuition, illustrating its significance across different contexts and its basis in both cognitive processes and neurological foundations.

# ABOUT THE AUTHOR

**<u>New Orleans Psychic Medium Cari Roy</u>**

New Orleans Psychic Medium Cari Roy has been featured on The Today Show twice, A&E, Discovery Plus, Biography and Travel Channels, local and national news and print. Recognized as New Orleans most accomplished psychic medium, she is a third generation spiritual practitioner making very fertile ground for her own abilities to develop. 40 years of professional experience have honed those abilities to skill. In addition to television appearances, Miss Roy is featured in documentaries about psychic development, has many published articles, is referenced in several books and is in demand for private readings, special events and speaking engagements. Miss Roy is named #1 Psychic Medium To See In New Orleans by travelchannel.com and is Recommended Best Psychic Medium To See In The USA by bbcamerica.com. "Awaken Your Intuition: Empowering Women For Success In Life & Business" is her first book and the start in a 6 book partnership with Mojo Rising Media. In her spare time Miss Roy is the proud mamma of 3 rescue animals and an advocate for animal rights and shelters. She also mentors, when possible, young readers who are developing their abilities. We are a woman owned and operated business and are active members of New Orleans & Company and the New Orleans Chamber of Commerce. For all enquiries please contact info@neworleanspsychic.com or queries@mojorisingmedia.com .